AN EQUITY BLUEPRINT

Actionable Strategies for Empowering Communities and Closing Opportunity Gaps

Dr. Eloisa Klementich

This book is dedicated to all whose shoulders I have been able to stand on. Your work, commitment and dedication to community have changed how I see and build history with purpose and heart.

Drew and Kelly, you both have been with me every step of the way, thank you.

For all those amazing, dedicated individuals I have had the pleasure to work and serve with, thank you. There is no doubt that I could not have written this book had you not come into my life.

To my daughters who challenged me to stand up and make my voice heard, my husband who has been my rock, my family and friends, thank you. Your belief in me has changed not only how I see the world, but how I strive to make a difference within it.

My amazing mother who is the wind beneath me, thank you.

And for those who continue to inspire me, thank you.

Stay in touch by going to my website   dreloisaklementich.org

"Our lives begin to end the day we become silent about things that matter"

"Be brave to stand for what you believe in even if you stand alone"

DR. MARTIN LUTHER KING JR.

CONTENTS

HOW TO USE THIS BOOK

An Equity Blueprint is organized to guide you from foundational concepts, practical application to a model for moving the needle in a community.

• Part I: Understanding Equity- introduces the core principles of equity and the historical context that shapes today's challenges. Due to the size of the literature already in existence, this section is not meant to be a comprehensive study but rather a high level look at why this is issue is a persistent problem still impacting community work today.

• Part II: Designing Effective Programs- presents actionable strategies, frameworks, metrics, tools and implementation strategies for advancing equity in a community.

• Part III: Case Studies- offers real-world case studies that illustrate how these strategies have been implemented across diverse settings and the lessons learned from a practitioner's point of view.

• Part IV: Personal Perspective- provides insight into a professional's lifelong curiosity, commitment to service, and the belief that thoughtful planning can transform lives and communities.

Each Part concludes with key takeaways to help you apply what you've learned. You can read the book cover to cover or jump directly to the sections most relevant to your work.

INTRODUCTION

Inequity remains a persistent and significant challenge in the United States, woven into the fabric of our history and institutions. Despite decades of progress, disparities in opportunity, wealth, health, and justice continue to shape the lives of millions. Addressing equity is not a simple task; it demands a nuanced understanding of the complex, intergenerational forces that have created and sustained these divides. To move forward, we must confront uncomfortable truths about our past and present by making deliberate choices about the future we wish to build.

The legacy of inequity is visible in countless aspects of American life. For example, the practice of changing street names at intersections to demarcate segregated neighborhoods stands as a stark reminder of how policy and place have been used to reinforce social boundaries. While such overt practices may have ended, their echoes persist in the economic, educational, and social divides that remain. Today, a convergence of historical reflection and economic realities has brought renewed attention to these disparities, prompting communities and leaders to ask difficult questions: Why do these gaps persist? Who benefits from the status quo? And what can be done to create a more just and equitable society?

This book is grounded in the belief that understanding the roots of inequity is essential to designing effective solutions. It examines the actions and omissions of early policymakers—decisions that, whether intentional or not, have shaped the opportunities available to different groups for generations. From slavery and emancipation to relocation policies and internment camps, the American story is marked by policies that have both harmed and, at times, sought to heal. As our collective understanding of these histories deepens, so too does the conversation about remedies and reparative action.

Yet, despite the growing awareness of inequity's costs, national urgency to address these issues remains limited to nonexistent. Too often, the responsibility for change is left to those most affected by injustice, while broader society hesitates to commit the resources and resolve needed for transformation. Research and experience, however, make clear that programs and policies promoting equity are not only necessary—but more importantly, they are effective when looking to improve the quality of neighborhoods. The challenge lies in identifying strategies that work, adapting them to local contexts, and sustaining the commitment required for lasting change.

Progress, while sometimes slow, is possible. Across the country, communities have demonstrated that targeted investments, collaborative partnerships, and responsive engagement can yield meaningful results. Local initiatives—whether focused on education, health, housing, community or economic development—have the power to spark broader movements, inspiring others and building momentum for systemic change. Let us be clear, no single program or policy can resolve all inequities, but coordinated, community-driven, people focused efforts can lay the foundation for a more equitable future.

This book offers a practical blueprint for those seeking to advance equity in their own communities. Drawing on case studies from across the nation and beyond, it provides strategic guidance, actionable tools, proven programs and adaptable frameworks designed to meet the unique needs of diverse settings.

Recognizing that every community faces its own challenges and opportunities, the book emphasizes flexibility, collaboration, persistence and the importance of local leadership.

At the heart of effective equity work is a commitment to partnership and shared responsibility. By engaging community members, organizations, and policymakers in the process, we can ensure that solutions are both responsive and sustainable. Supporting historically underserved populations and promoting equitable opportunities benefits not only those directly affected, but the entire community—driving economic growth, social cohesion, and a stronger sense of shared purpose.

For readers committed to making a difference, this book is both a call to action and a practical blueprint. It invites you to reflect on the roots of inequity, to learn from the successes and challenges of others, and to join a growing movement dedicated to building a more just and inclusive society. Through sustained effort, thoughtful planning, and unwavering commitment, lasting change is not only possible—it is within our reach.

PREFACE

Equity fundamentally involves addressing individual circumstances to ensure that all persons have equal access to opportunities for success, regardless of their background, ethnicity, financial circumstances, or geographic location. Ideally, specialized programs are created in the very areas of an individual's need to ensure their success. However, this approach presents a significant challenge: how to design programs that can generate positive outcomes across entire communities while meeting individuals where they are. This book provides an actionable blueprint for programs and policies that can drive the success communities are in search of. Drawing on three decades of experience in economic development and community investment, this work consolidates successful methodologies, best practices, and encountered challenges from national and international contexts.

Achieving equity requires a deliberate, collaborative, and persistent approach. Sustainable change necessitates commitment at all levels of government and involvement by civil society to review and implement policies, programs, and processes capable of altering community trajectories to an aligned vision. This book presents a comprehensive blueprint for anyone doing this type of work so that they can reference actionable case studies, practical insights, and innovative strategies designed to advance nationwide efforts to close equity gaps.

PART 1:

AN URGENT CONVERSATION

The divide between rich and poor in America is not just a theoretical or social conversation but rather is one rooted in data and that data is very clear. The divide between the rich and poor is widening, with income inequality now at historic highs. According to the National Bureau of Economic Research, the top 1% hold as much wealth as the bottom 90%. By the same token, the Pew Research Institute found that middle-income households decreased from 61% in 1971 to 51% in 2019 [1]. This indicates that a significant proportion of wealth is concentrated among the affluent, while numerous former middle-class families are experiencing economic decline.

The Pew Research Institute's data indicates a modest increase in the proportion of adults at the upper-income level, suggesting that some individuals from the middle class may have transitioned into higher income brackets. While there are incremental advancements in upward mobility, the research also highlights that income growth rates differ across various income groups. For example, from 1970 to 2018 the middle-class income growth rate was 49% and the lower-income growth rate was 43%, which is lower than the upper-tier income growth rate of 64%.[2] To provide context, the lower-income tier saw an income increase of just $8,700 over 48 years (1970 to 2018), which has not kept pace with inflation. Additionally, the median net worth of families declined by 40% from its peak in 2007.

The recognition of wealth inequality has also been highlighted in the World Economic Forum Reports. They highlight that the top 10% of the global population receive about 52% of the global income while the bottom 50% receive only 8%. To put this in perspective the salary for the top 10% is about $122,100 while the individual at the bottom half will earn just $3,920. In terms of accumulated assets not just income, the divide is even larger where the top 10% own about 75% of the global wealth while the bottom 50% own just 2%. The average income gap between the top 10% and the bottom 50% of individuals within countries has seen a similar trend of doubling across the same period.[3]

In *Capital in the Twenty-First Century*, Thomas Piketty, a professor at the Paris School of Economics, highlights the concentration of wealth among the few is driving a return on capital that is greater than the rate of economic growth – a phenomenon behind some of the "social and economic instability" and the extremisms in many countries today. We have become a society with a zero-sum game mentality.[4] Basically, if you're not with me, you're against me. This mindset perpetuates income inequality even more.

According to Piketty and other researchers, income inequality results from the combined effect of various policies over time rather than the actions of a single individual or policy. Factors such as globalization, technological advancements, the value of the minimum wage, investments in education, taxation rates, and union representation contribute to economic inequality. Because multiple factors influence economic inequality, addressing it requires a comprehensive approach across different policy areas and levels of government for lasting effects.

As community focused practitioners and policy makers,

we must resist the desire for fast results, not only do the systematic issues play a strong role but also the Volatility, Uncertainty, Complexity, and Ambiguity (VUCA) world in which we live.[5] In other words, this effort will take years of focus and investment to change direction. In *The 2030 Agenda for Sustainable Development*, the United Nations is leading the path for an international plan of action for a stronger people, planet and prosperity. Within this work, they highlight the need to "realize the human rights of all and to achieve gender equality."[6] While all 17 Sustainable Development Goals matter, Goal 10, "Reduced Inequalities," is especially crucial as it directs national and international attention toward removing barriers and improving access for underserved communities. The United Nations encourages cities and regions to adopt equitable policies and invest in programs that can reduce income inequality both globally and nationally.

While many federal governments consider options like progressive wealth taxes or baby bonds to address wealth inequality, this book targets frontline workers in government, philanthropy, nonprofit, and business sectors who drive equitable economic development and community investment. Their focused efforts and programs can create meaningful, lasting change for families and communities. Though progress may be gradual, these initiatives help build stronger communities where everyone has the opportunity to pursue happiness, regardless of race or economic status.

The Founding of America

The United States was established by a group of leaders commonly referred to as the Founding Fathers. Following the American Revolution, these individuals focused their efforts on creating a new nation-state.[7] While the precise structure of the country's future political system remained uncertain, there was consensus on several points: the rejection of monarchy, liberty, and any form of special privileges for individuals or groups.

The government would be tasked with safeguarding individual rights, and a nation-state would be established to resolve interstate disputes. However, issues such as taxation, slavery, and the role of religion were still under consideration.

Since these individuals all came together with their own experiences, beliefs and practices, it was critical that they align on what unified their efforts. Education was one of those areas that the founders believed was universally needed as it would support the newly established democracy, could serve as a means out of poverty and drive larger economic-social opportunity. Drawing on their work, I believe, increased income inequality across any demographic group does not align with widely held ideals about equal opportunity in the United States. While the Civil War, the Lincoln Presidency, and the 14th Amendment were important in advancing these principles, it truly was the Bill of Rights that established the fundamental protection of liberties and asserts that all individuals are created equal.[8] The statement "all men [individuals] are created equal" holds significant influence and is intended to guide the nation's principles. The phrase "all men" encompasses all individuals, regardless of race, ethnicity, sexual orientation, gender, location, wealth, or education. The Constitution explicitly guarantees every person the right to "life, liberty and the pursuit of happiness." According to these constitutional ideals, every individual should be afforded an opportunity to aspire and to pursue their ambitions.

In Martin Luther King's sermon delivered at Ebenezer Baptist Church in Atlanta, Georgia on July 4, 1965, he too rang the bell, noting our God-given rights. He called for us to "respect the dignity and the worth of all human personality," emphasizing that a job, with a decent wage, provides dignity and the means to support a family. He asserted the only way to make the American Dream work is to rid the country of segregation and discrimination.

These civil liberties serve as the cornerstone of the nation's constitution and are also safeguarded by the Bill of Rights. They encompass freedoms such as speech, press, and religion. Both documents lay the groundwork for a more inclusive and accessible government, offering opportunities to all residents and workers within the country.

The principles of equal access and opportunity are fundamental to building a society where individuals and families can lead fulfilling lives. However, despite these ideals, many Americans still encounter significant barriers that prevent them from fully realizing the promise of the American Dream. Understanding the reasons behind these persistent obstacles is essential for creating more inclusive and equitable communities.

Whose American Dream

Dr. King asserted that "if the American Dream is to be a reality, we must work to make it a reality and realize the urgency of the moment." Upon relocating to Atlanta, I attended a forum at the historic Ebenezer Baptist Church, where Dr. Bernice King, Kwanza Hall, and Al Vivian—all children of prominent civil rights leaders—discussed the significance and impact of the movement. The event provided valuable insights into the historical legacy and the considerable personal contributions made by these individuals and their families for the collective advancement of their community and this nation.

The term "American Dream" originated in 1931, introduced by James Truslow Adams in his book *The Epic of America*. Like much of history, this concept has evolved over time; today, its definition often encompasses elements of economic opportunity and social mobility, suggesting that any individual can aspire to achieve success regardless of socioeconomic background. The enduring nature of this idea can be traced back to the nation's founding principles. Nonetheless, it remains critical to continually examine how each generation interprets and pursues this ideal, as societal goals and interests inevitably change over time.

As Dr. King aptly stated, "I haven't lost the faith, I still have a dream ... this morning that truth will reign supreme and all of God's children will respect the dignity and worth of human personality." The ongoing commitment to the vision for justice and inclusivity requires continued advocacy and perseverance, recognizing that progress is gradual and the effort is ongoing. This endeavor is not solely the responsibility of legislators, economic development professionals, philanthropists, or community advocates; rather, it demands collective participation from all citizens to pursue and safeguard the fundamental liberties to which everyone is entitled.

Ambassador Andrew Young is widely recognized for his significant contributions to advancing human rights and civil liberties. Throughout his career, he has dedicated himself to supporting individuals facing disenfranchisement both nationally and internationally. With firsthand experience of persecution and a deep understanding of socio-economic challenges, Ambassador Young has consistently advocated for equal rights.

During our meeting, the Ambassador reflected on his involvement in bringing the Olympics to Atlanta, his tenure as Mayor, his initiatives in Africa, and Dr. Martin Luther King Jr.'s Nobel Peace Prize.[9] While each topic was very informative, his remarks concerning the ongoing pursuit of Dr. King's vision of a Beloved Community were particularly noteworthy, prompting detailed reflection. Ambassador Young went on to explain that for Dr. King, the Beloved Community would be without poverty, hunger, and homeless. It would be a community that would resolve any differences in a peaceful, cooperative, and respectful manner.[10]

Based on my conversation with Ambassador Young, it is clear that the concept of the Beloved Community is deeply rooted in economic empowerment for all individuals. While this idea has significant historical context, it remains highly relevant today and provides a strong foundation for developing future strategies. Ambassador Young has dedicated a distinguished career to advancing economic inclusivity—not only in Atlanta, but across the United States and in Africa. Ambassador Young's leadership is marked by a commitment to building connections among people and communities, rather than fostering division. The positive influence of these efforts is evident throughout the City of Atlanta and its broader environment.

As our meeting concluded, I requested guidance from Ambassador Young regarding priorities for the next generation aiming to achieve enduring success for everyone. He offered concise yet profound advice: "Do not give up." He emphasized that countless individuals before me have made significant sacrifices for their beliefs and that efforts to address income inequality are crucial for realizing the vision of a Beloved Community. The journey toward this goal is challenging but fundamentally worthwhile, extending beyond Atlanta to impact the nation and the world.

My engagement with Ambassador Young was both professionally and personally very meaningful, shaping my perspectives and strengthening my commitment to equity. The conversation reinforced that every contribution, regardless of scale, builds upon prior efforts and collectively drives sustained community transformation.

Hence, I have come to the conclusion that an individual's American Dream cannot be achieved alone or by any single organization; it requires unified action from all stakeholders. Only through the collective efforts of the entire community can we effect meaningful change within neighborhoods, communities, and for each individual. The American Dream becomes attainable when we come together to uplift and support one another.

Unified action means:

- **Collaborative partnerships** between local government, businesses, nonprofits, and residents to address shared challenges.
- **Community engagement** that ensures all voices are heard and included in decision-making.
- **Resource sharing**, such as pooling expertise, funding,

and networks to maximize impact.

- **Advocacy for equitable policies** that remove barriers and expand opportunities for all.
- **Support systems** that provide mentorship, education, and access to essential services for those in need.

When each stakeholder commits to working together—sharing responsibility, listening actively, and acting with purpose—we create the conditions for everyone to pursue and achieve their own American Dream.

Equity and Equality

The distinction between equality and equity is frequently misunderstood or incorrectly defined. Although the difference may seem minor, each perspective profoundly influences policy development and program implementation. When designing equitable initiatives, the primary objective is to ensure that all individuals have access to opportunities, whether related to funding, programming, or broader ecosystems. For example, in establishing an equitable grant process, an organization might consider sharing the evaluation criteria, making applications accessible online, and notifying all businesses of the opportunity. These measures are often perceived as sufficient for inclusive participation but in practicality, they are not. More intentionality is needed to engage the business in an underserved community.

One of the most notable advertisements produced during my tenure at the State of California Business, Transportation and Housing Agency was "Our Garages are where ideas are made." California is often recognized for its association with innovation, particularly within hubs such as San Diego, San Francisco, and Silicon Valley, which collectively cover approximately 2,300 mi^2. In contrast, other areas of the state—spanning 161,400 mi^2—do not have a comparable concentration of angel and venture capital or established innovation ecosystems. Cities like San Fernando, Calexico, and Susanville, while notable, do not possess as strong innovation infrastructures. Establishing robust innovation ecosystems typically involves multiple components including universities, financial capital, and entrepreneurs. At that time, there was an effort to encourage the growth of innovation beyond the traditional hubs within the state.

The Department of Energy's National Laboratories consist of 17 institutions with a total of 19 complexes across the United States. Notably, California houses four of these complexes—double the number found in any other state, as three states each have two locations. It became evident that despite California's reputation for innovation and possessing a robust innovation ecosystem, not all regions within the state benefited equally or fully perceived these advantages. Recognizing the untapped potential statewide, particularly with respect to leveraging key assets such as the National Laboratories, we established the State's Innovation Hubs. These Hubs were designed to target additional cities and regions endowed with critical resources that, if cultivated and utilized, could drive the growth and consolidation of innovation communities. While the Innovation Hub initiative is not a comprehensive solution, it has provided a valuable platform—a forum for discussion and collaboration concerning the economic impact of innovation. The program, though continuously evolving, remains active to this day.

This approach underscores the significance of equity. Communities that prioritize equity foster safe environments with access to quality education, nutritious food, healthcare services, promising employment opportunities, safe neighborhoods and affordable housing. These components interact to build resilient communities and provide individuals with avenues for generational wealth creation. Fundamentally, equity involves meeting individuals and businesses where they are; achieving this requires understanding their circumstances and incorporating essential elements into program design to ensure active participation. For instance, when reviewing previous grant programs, it is important to assess not only procedural steps but also how announcements reach potential applicants, whether applications are accessible in multiple languages, insurance requirements, clarity of other requirements, and provision of technical assistance. Identifying and addressing unintended barriers within the grant process is crucial to ensuring the intended beneficiaries have genuine access to opportunities.

In Atlanta, my organization had the responsibility of distributing Federal CARES Act funds to businesses. Several valuable lessons emerged from this experience, particularly regarding application completion rates. Upon reviewing incomplete submissions, we observed that approximately 30% stalled at the penultimate step, which required submission of business financials. To better understand this issue, we conducted a survey of all incomplete applicants who responded, revealing that many did not have their financial records adequately prepared. While it may not fall within the purview of government agencies to manage private business finances, truly equitable programs must include support mechanisms—such as financial consultation and technical assistance—to enable targeted businesses not only to be notified of the opportunity, be able to complete the application but also to strengthen their capacity for long-term success within the community.

Advancing equity requires more than the creation of equitable programs; it demands a commitment to fostering an equitable mindset. Achieving sustainable community impact necessitates intentional strategies that promote full inclusion and participation, ensuring that benefits are realized and shared by the target audience whether a business, community group and/or resident.

Why Equity Matters

What history and data has proved is that a rising tide does not lift all boats; that is, unless there is a deliberate and focused effort to do so. In the United States the rising tide has come to a limited number of people, leaving many, particularly the global majority, in difficult economic situations. Economist and *New York Times* columnist Paul Krugman noted that not only is an unequal society – income inequality – undemocratic with unequal access to opportunity and outcome but that an unequal society drives a class-dominated politics.[11] This is precisely why equity matters – it's not only about giving everyone access to opportunity but, I believe it, drives to the heart of this countries existence – we are a country built on the right to freedoms and access to tailored opportunities driving outcomes that are fair not just the starting point.

From 1964 to 1968, Lyndon Johnson implemented many programs known as the "Great Society" in effort to eliminate poverty, reduce racial injustice and expand social welfare. These programs included Head Start, Medicare and War on Poverty, all good examples of the federal government trying to ameliorate disparities. Recognizing that no program is perfect, I believe you can understand President Johnson's overall intent and his thinking on equity, just turn to his 1965 speech at Howard University. He said, "You do not take a person who has been hobbled by chains and bring him up to the starting line of a race, and then say, 'you are free to compete with all the others,' and still justly believe that you have been fair." In my opinion, he understood that equity required more than equal access but intentionality to give people what they needed to ensure they could partake in all that the country had to offer.

At the age of five, my parents made the decision to transfer my siblings and me from our local public school to a private Christian school located approximately 25 minutes from our home. This transition necessitated my mother to re-enter the workforce, reflecting their personal commitment to investing in our education. Although neither parent had attended college, they recognized the transformative potential that education could provide for their children. For my parents, education would be our path to equity. In fact, for many minority communities, education serves as a pathway to enhanced opportunities, resources and beneficial outcomes. However, this option is not accessible to all families, as the necessary sacrifices can be prohibitive, resulting in limited opportunities for some individuals.

It is widely understood that the ability to work is closely tied to a person's economic mobility potential, the well-being of the family and their life outcomes. At the same time, access to affordable workforce housing is imperative to the success of maintaining that job and stability for many families. Even though this is understood, often the affordable housing units are not near a city's job center. Although cost is a major challenge, affordable housing far from work often decreases the economic impact for the employee. In 2017, my analysis of Atlanta showed that moderate-income households spend about 63% of their income on housing and transportation—roughly $11 billion for families near job centers. If cities help families live closer to work and cut these costs by just 5%, it could return $550 million to household budgets, boosting both the local economy and equity. In other words, there is no question that affordable housing is needed throughout a city. Rather, affordable housing units increase their effectiveness when they are by a job center as they lower an individual's spend on transportation and time.

Programs and Policies that Drove Inequalities

Historical policies and practices have significantly influenced communities of color, often placing them at the forefront of systemic inequality. Addressing these longstanding impacts presents substantial challenges, as their effects have accumulated over many years and require sustained effort to alter their course.

While certain government programs and policies may have been established with different objectives, their overall impact on affected communities has been negative, contributing to persistent disparities. An illustrative example is housing policy; affordable housing continues to be a priority for policymakers, much as it was following the Great Depression. At that time, the federal government developed agencies such as the Homeowners Loan Corporation (HOLC) and the Federal Housing Administration (FHA), both intended to promote homeownership.

In particular, the HOLC offered struggling homeowners refinancing assistance by purchasing the mortgage and then reissuing amortized mortgages with longer repayment schedules.[12] In addition, FHA would underwrite mortgage risk with the intent of spurring banks to lend more funds to potential homeowners.

The results of these efforts were the creation of "residential security" maps by HOLC and FHA. In essence, these maps ranked neighborhoods based on their risk and creditworthiness. The term "redlining" comes from the color-coded map for the "D" grade areas that meant these red areas were considered as hazards and credit unworthy. It was no coincidence that among the factors considered in grading the areas of the map were neighborhood residents' race and ethnicity, with people of color and of Jewish descent considered detrimental to a neighborhood.

Not only did this practice strengthen residential segregation but it also made favorable loan terms unattainable for minorities. What is even more disheartening is that according to The National Center for Biotechnology Information, many of these same redlined areas, continue to experience "higher poverty, vacancy rates, risk of loan denials, subprime lending, and mortgage default, and lower economic mobility, homeownership rates, and home values."[13] In fact, Bloomberg highlighted that "the redlined areas today generally remain more segregated and more economically disadvantaged, with higher Black and minority shares of population than the remainder of the city."[14]

Other policies that targeted particular groups with enduring negative economic impacts include examples such as slavery, Japanese Exclusion Act, Indian Removal Act, denial to the GI benefits (particularly for African Americans) and the Mexican Farm Labor Act. Recognizing the tremendous economic loss these policies caused and the negative impacts they have brought to future generations, a brief conversation here would not do this part of the U.S. history justice; hence, I have decided to come back to each of these events at another time. With that said, the devasting impacts of these policies are real.

For example, the Japanese Exclusion Act impacted some 120,000 Japanese Americans, about two thirds were full citizens, born and raised in the U.S. With the signing of Executive Order 9066, President Roosevelt directed the War Department to create war areas or relocation areas for people of Japanese descent. These individuals lost some $400 million in property during their incarceration.[15]

It is also important to highlight the impact of labor unions in the income inequality conversation. Starting after World War II until the 1970s, the labor movement saw a doubling of median compensation and labor productivity representing sustained prosperity, which was shared among the workers.[16] And yet from 1978-2011 union membership declined by 12.6% to 11.3% -- a decline that brought, by some estimates, about a third of the increase in inequality. In fact, labor productivity has almost doubled since 1973 while during the same time median wages have seen only a 4% increase.[17]

Lastly, even though the federal tax policy has not increased income inequality, it has not done much to combat it. The federal tax policy has seen declines in the top marginal tax rate, which is a tax on the wealthiest individuals and overall tax cuts. Even though the United States has a progressive tax system, which in theory reduces income inequality, the lower tax rates offset any potential impact to income inequality leaving the opportunity for lasting impact missed.[18]

The initial step in addressing inequity involves recognizing the issue and formulating a strategic plan that details targeted actions to resolve challenges faced by communities of color and other underserved groups. Professionals engaged in economic and community development, as well as those working within nonprofit organizations, share a commitment to creating positive economic outcomes for the populations they serve. This impact is fundamental to promoting economic vitality, fostering empowerment, and advancing economic justice. Economic justice is characterized by universal access to quality education, safe environments, plentiful resources, and opportunities for personal fulfilment.

As a nation, we still pursue happiness, but achieving the American Dream now depends on programs and policies that ensure equitable access. The next generation seeks fairness for communities, the environment, and businesses in response to past injustices.

Equity by the Numbers

In a joint study, University of Bonn and Princeton University found that Black Americans in 2019 held 1/6 the per capita wealth of White Americans. It goes on to state that this percentage is smaller than that of the 1980s[19]. More recent work by Blanchet, Saez and Zucman with Realtime Inequality, found that by then end of 2021, "adults in the top .1% controlled almost 19% of the U.S. wealth, up from 7% in 1976...[while] Black Americans, on average, earned $48,000 in 2021, about half as much as those who are White."[20]

Every year the American Community Survey, driven by the U.S. Census Bureau, updates its data to give governments and decisionmakers a complete and accurate picture of today's society when they create policy. *Income and Poverty in the United States: 2020 Report* is one such report that provides remarkable insight into income inequality in the U.S. and the country's waning ability to effectively address it[21].

- For the first time since 2011, the 2020 median household income actually declined from the 2019 of $69,560 to $67,521, representing a 2.9% decrease for Americans.
- There was a decrease in the real median earning for all workers aged 15 and over with earnings, as income levels decreased from $42,065 in 2019 to $41,535 in 2020.
- After five years of improvement, the country's poverty rate also increased in 2020 by 1% to 11.4% from 10.5%.

The report examines racial groups across the country's poverty rate, noting a higher concentration of poverty among Blacks, with the highest poverty rate (19.5%) and Hispanics (17%).

It also finds an increase in poverty rates among non-Hispanic Whites (8.2%).

Looking at the rate based on married-couple families and families who are supported by a female householder, there were also increases. In particular, the poverty rate for married couple families increased from 4% in 2019 to 4.7% in 2020 whereas a female householder's poverty increase jumped by 1.2% from 22.2 in 2019 to 23.4% in 2020.

The data reveals that the income inequality impact exists across all racial groups. No question that the impacts are more significant for the minority groups, but it is also felt among non-Hispanic Whites.

The U.S. Department of Agriculture reported that across all races, the U.S. poverty rate in 2019 was 15.4% higher in rural areas when compared to metro areas, which had an 11.9% poverty rate.[22] Here, too, the data shows that 30.7% of Blacks had the highest incidence of poverty in 2019. If you compare the Black rate of poverty for that same year in urban areas, although higher than other races, there is a decrease to 20.4%.

The second highest poverty rate is among American Indians and Alaska Natives at 29.6%. Yet again, when looking at the same population race in urban areas, although high, the rate decreases to 19.4%. When considering White residents in rural America, the 2019 poverty rate was 13.3% in rural areas compared to 9.7% in the urban core.

Lastly, Hispanics did not fare any better, they are the third group experiencing the highest level of poverty and are seeing the same trend. In rural America, the poverty rates among Hispanics in 2019 was 21.7% compared with 16.9% in urban areas.

It would be important to note that time has not made a statistical difference for the country's poverty rate. In the Poverty in the United States: 2023 report, it showed that the official poverty rate decreased slightly by 0.4 percentage points to 10.6% representing 35.9 million people.[23] The lack of movement in these metrics confirms the byzantine challenge facing policymakers and an even greater one for practitioners. In the end, we need to design policies and programs that effectively address increasing concentrations of poverty across different racial groups and geographic locations, thereby providing benefits to the largest possible population.

Key Takeaways for Part 1

To advance equity in your community, start by designing programs with empathy—listen deeply to the lived experiences of those you serve and tailor support to meet both individual and collective needs. Use intentional outreach strategies that leverage multiple channels and adapt to cultural and linguistic differences, ensuring everyone can access opportunities. Regularly evaluate your programs, seek honest feedback, and be open to refining your approach as circumstances change. Embrace innovation and collaboration across sectors, combining data-driven insights with personal stories to guide decisions and measure impact. Most importantly, empower communities by engaging stakeholders authentically, making their voices central to every initiative, and fostering a culture of continuous improvement. By integrating these principles, you can create responsive, inclusive, and sustainable solutions that close opportunity gaps and help all community members thrive.

PART II:

MEETING PEOPLE WHERE THEY ARE

Developing programs aimed at promoting equity involves engaging individuals according to their specific needs and circumstances to drive positive outcomes. This includes offering services and programs designed to facilitate their success, however that may be defined. Outreach, in this context, refers to providing support through tailored methods. For example, when designing a program for seniors, simply sending a postcard to all seniors in the community may not be sufficient. Instead, outreach may include attending senior events, assisting with form completion, detailed 'how to' videos and making forms available both in handwritten and online formats. Since some seniors may not prefer or be able to complete forms online, caregivers might need to assist; caregivers often work during the day, so it is important to provide options for easy and efficient submission at all hours of the day. These examples illustrate approaches to supporting the principle of addressing individuals' varied needs. Fundamentally, this strategy involves understanding the intended audience and employing deliberate methods to engage them, similar to how businesses tailor strategies to reach their key consumers and customer segments.

Since this country's founding, there has been a prevailing expectation that diligent work enables individuals to build their reputations and support their families, an ethos commonly referred to as "pulling yourself up by your bootstraps." Today, this expectation is amplified as younger generations increasingly advocate for equitable access to all opportunities. In fact, younger generations are demanding their voices be heard in this conversation. An October 2020 C.S. Mott Children's Hospital National Poll on Children's Health at Michigan Medicine found that one in twelve parents reported their teenager had participated in a demonstration or related event concerning racism or policing reform.[24]

The central challenge lies in developing programs that address individuals' specific needs while simultaneously generating significant impact across the broader community to reduce inequality. Providing tailored support is inherently demanding—requiring substantial time, human resources, and financial investment—but remains essential for addressing disparities within society. Consequently, establishing a service and program delivery model that integrates personalized attention within an equity-at-scale framework offers a viable solution. This book proposes strategies to achieve this dual objective. With the collective engagement of individuals, organizations, civil society and governmental bodies dedicated to advancing equity, there is an opportunity to foster a community that supports sustainable progress. It is important to acknowledge that implementing equity-focused initiatives yields gradual results; meaningful change will be incremental and requires sustained commitment. The subsequent chapters will provide comprehensive details and practical guidance regarding these approaches.

What Are We Solving For

Local governments, civil society and community-focused

organizations possess the capacity, commitment and passion to address numerous inequities and can significantly influence individuals' lives.

Problem-Solving

The process begins by acknowledging the existence of an issue—in this instance, that policies and programs implemented by governing bodies have contributed to persistent inequalities affecting certain population groups within the community. Frequently, subsequent programs and policies compound these disparities, further marginalizing vulnerable groups. The primary objective is to address inequity, striving to reduce and ultimately eliminate it. While this may appear straightforward and some organizations may adapt readily, others may require several months to recognize challenges and coordinate responsive efforts.

Identifying problems within a community is inherently complex, as perspectives vary; some individuals may not perceive any existing issues due to personal achievements or life opportunities. To complicate the issue, contemporary American culture often promotes the concept of "pulling oneself up by the bootstraps". Interestingly, when the phrase first emerged in the 1800s, it conveyed an entirely different meaning than its current interpretation. In fact, as described by Nicholas Kristof in his opinion piece in the *New York Times*, the term was first to describe "an impossible act."[25] But today, the term means one can achieve success without the help of anyone else but their own grit and determination. This is not to say that there are not individuals who have come from humble and difficult beginnings that have achieved great success, but this notion is not the norm for most Americans. Typically, it takes "a village", as highlighted in the Nigerian Igbo culture, to ensure the success of an individual.

During a neighborhood meeting, I observed an attendee express the view that Affirmative Action programs for college students were inefficient and unfair to white students with higher grades. Although I did not concur with this perspective, I acknowledged the importance of listening during such discussions, so I refrained from commenting, initially. The individual proceeded to discuss various community matters before returning to Affirmative Action, asserting that most beneficiaries of these programs fail in college anyway.

Recognizing that this was only one person feeling, I had to say something. So, when it was my opportunity to speak, I addressed the topic by noting that each person's path to higher education is unique. Personally, Affirmative Action provided access to college. I clarified that while the program offered an entry point, success required dedication to attending classes and fulfilling all academic responsibilities. As the first member of my family to attend a four-year institution, I eventually completed undergraduate through doctoral studies. I emphasized that college presents challenges for all students, and for many, it serves as a means of economic advancement for themselves and their families – me included.

In fact, in the *Educational Evaluation and Policy Analysis Journal*, Heather Rose looked at the graduation rates of those admitted through Affirmative Action programs. She found that 57% of Affirmative Action students graduated compared to 73% of non-Affirmative Action students, which is only a 16% difference. She also looked at those students just above the regular admissions cutoff graduation rates compared to affirmative action students. Here she found that graduation rates were only 8 percentage points different.[26]

Since the passage of the Wagner Act in 1935 under the Roosevelt Administration, there have been notable changes in administrative policies. Historical evidence demonstrates that policy decisions significantly influence the populations they are designed to protect. Therefore, addressing economic inequalities most effectively requires deliberate policy reform. However, as some parties remain unconvinced of the existence of these disparities, those who recognize the need for corrective measures can initiate equity strategies independently. These initiatives may be implemented at various levels, including regions, cities, or states. As communities engage in these efforts, broader understanding and support for such approaches will likely emerge, encouraging wider participation. Now is the opportune moment to advance meaningful actions toward enhancing economic mobility.

Revaluation of Current Programs

As practitioners, it is essential to implement best-in-class programs. However, since communities evolve and their needs change, it is vital to approach the work with humility and recognize that initial solutions may not always be optimal throughout time. A program that was appropriate at a specific time may no longer suit the changing needs of a community or individual; therefore, maintaining relevance requires periodic reassessment and adaptation of these programs. Continuous learning from past mistakes, openness to necessary adjustments, and iterative exploration of effective strategies are all key elements to success. Additionally, what proves effective one year or in a particular community may not be suitable in another context. Acknowledging that people and communities are dynamic underscores the importance for practitioners to consistently re-evaluate programs, monitor results, analyze shortcomings, and demonstrate agility in response to new insights. An objective review of program performance enables agencies to identify areas for modification and improvement.

Self-assessment can present difficulties due to established relationships within teams or resistance to altering established routines. Maintaining the status quo may seem convenient as it avoids updating documents, processes, and procedures; however, this approach can impede progress. Experience has shown that overconfidence can hinder critical evaluation and necessary safeguards. Just as thorough checks are indispensable in high-risk activities, so too is continuous assessment crucial in program administration. The risk of not regularly evaluating a program's effectiveness could potentially undermine community and economic development, benefit, and equitable access.

To ensure objectivity, organizations could/should periodically seek external reviews of their programs, processes, and impact. For smaller organizations where this may not be feasible, internally identifying the most innovative staff—regardless of department—and assigning them this responsibility can provide fresh perspectives. It is vital that these efforts are grounded in a clear purpose: to enhance productivity and service capacity, not to assign blame. External feedback does not necessarily require hiring consultants; often, the most valuable recommendations come directly from end-users through surveys and other forms of feedback. For example, collaboration with a small business lending team highlighted stakeholder concerns about requirements such as life insurance policies for loan closing. Upon investigation, it became evident that while these guidelines aimed to protect public funds, they also created barriers, especially for small businesses facing significant costs. Further research of this small business requirement indicated that over a 25-year period and more than 500 loans, recourse to a business owner's life insurance occurred only once. While providing an additional layer of protection, the requirement deterred more applicants than the number of cases it benefitted. This analysis prompted the organization to revise its policy: unless specifically required by the entity capitalizing the fund, life insurance is no longer mandatory for loan closure.

This case demonstrates the value of ongoing critical evaluation and responsiveness to stakeholder input. By removing unnecessary obstacles, the organization can both advance its mission and enhance positive outcomes for the community. When program modifications are informed by measured impact and community feedback, organizations are better position themselves to deliver inclusive growth and meaningful change.

Open to New

To successfully implement new ecosystem models, organizations must constantly adopt fresh tools and approaches to deliver relevant and sustainable solutions for both community and business needs. This process demands attention to funding, organizational structure, and often legal or board approvals. Success is rooted in intentional change, not habit.

Routine thinking can stifle creativity, mainly due to heavy workloads that leave little room for exploring new ideas. Scheduling dedicated time for reflection—such as reading articles, attending conference, or learning from other organizations—can spark innovation and ensure up-to-date strategies. To this end, embracing failure is necessary; no new program is perfect at launch, and iteration is key. Leaders should foster environments where experimentation is safe, and clear communication with boards helps mitigate risks associated with innovation.

Connecting with other leaders and organizations provides valuable inspiration and insights, leading to better programs through shared learning. Seeking out spaces—both physical and mental—where innovative thinking thrives is essential. For example, learning from James Bailey's achievements at the Russell Center for Innovation motivated changes in my own organization. The Russell Center for Innovation was established as a co-working space that opened their doors just months before COVID. Who would have ever known that their entire growth model would be paused due to a worldwide pandemic. And yet, through his vision and leadership, he was able to navigate the center through COVID to now being the national leader in "pursuing pathways to expand the possibilities for Black entrepreneurs in Atlanta and beyond at a time when ensuring equitable opportunities for Black-owned businesses matters more than ever. Black entrepreneurs require more than symbols of hope at this critical time. They need institutions to manufacture it. RICE will do our part– to help create and accelerate opportunities for Black business owners, bring them into a family of dynamic people like them, and surround them with everything they need to prosper."[27]

Inspiration can come from anywhere, but purposeful exploration, innovation and risk taking is vital for growth.

Strategy: The Role of Data

Certain individuals within communities benefit from existing systems and consequently perceive no issues with the status quo. These structures—whether in business or politics—have served their interests effectively, leading them to assume that those who have not experienced similar success may simply not have fully utilized available opportunities. In discussions with such stakeholders, addressing broader community realities is best accomplished through the presentation of data, research, and factual evidence.

Data plays an essential role in accurately illustrating and contextualizing the prevailing economic conditions. It serves as an impartial instrument for conveying reality and supporting meaningful dialogue. In fact, the Bureau of Labor estimates that the demand for research analysts is projected to grow 23% from 2022 to 2032 which would put the profession at a faster growth rate than the average occupation.[28] Data enables organizations to set benchmarks, guide discussions, track progress, and hold themselves accountable for their goals. While data metrics are useful, many are lagging indicators that reflect past performance; leading indicators predict future outcomes. Both data types are necessary for a balanced assessment, so it's critical to know which you are using and how they affect your objectives. For example, some lagging metrics from the U.S. government are updated infrequently, requiring awareness of their limitations.

Data alone doesn't tell the whole story—combine quantitative measures, which address amounts, with qualitative insights that explain underlying reasons with real life examples and/or explanatory stories. Present information in an accessible way, and reference data across national, regional, and local levels for context and comparison. Clarify your communication goals so data can truly inform your impact.

When choosing metrics to assess communities, consider your message, audience, and desired outcomes. Metrics exist almost for every measure and can include things like demographics, place, education, or economic conditions. The following examples reflect metrics I have used to analyze impact in disinvested neighborhoods. With that said, it is important to recognize that every community has unique needs and priorities. More on metrics will be picked up later in the book.

A Sample of Possible Metrics

Household Income	Violent Crime	Good Jobs	Early Learning
Joblessness	Vacant Commercial Properties	Workers obtaining benefits	Students Reading to Learn
Home Ownership	Commute Times	Business Creation	Access to Fresh Food
Access to Banking	High Educational Attainment	Small Business Survival Rates	Low Education Attainment
Housing Cost Burden	Proximity to Parks	SB Formation	Access to Vehicles
Students on Track for College	Free and Reduced Price School Meals	Workers earning a livable wage	No.of Affordable Housing Units
Community Engagement	Truancy Rates	Housing Units	Disposal Income

Figure 2.1 A sample of possible metrics

Make It Personal

Incorporating the experiences of individuals affected by challenges introduces a vital human dimension when advocating for change. Personal narratives serve to contextualize data, illustrating its impact on real lives. For example, I recall Mrs. Betty, an elderly woman who fulfilled her aspiration of homeownership at age 82, enabled by a down payment assistance program. After completing the required course and saving diligently, she was able to purchase her first home. The joy she expressed upon receiving her keys was a testament to the transformative power of such initiatives, inspiring not only the team but also others with similar ambitions.

While data itself remains objective, it is essential to remind stakeholders that behind every statistic are individuals—our friends, family, neighbors, and colleagues—which brings necessary perspective to discussions about policy and outcomes. Data illustrates the impact in real terms; stories illustrate the impact to people who are just like you.

It is also important for these stories to reflect the diversity within communities, representing varied ethnicities and socioeconomic backgrounds to ensure a comprehensive understanding. For instance, I encountered a small business owner who struggled to secure investment until he accessed a city loan program. This opportunity allowed him to transition from operating a food truck to opening multiple restaurant locations, realizing his goal of sharing his mother's Indian recipes with a wider audience. The support provided by the loan was instrumental in changing the trajectory of his business, family and his life.

Developing more equitable programs and policies necessitates engaging all stakeholders to collaboratively seek solutions. In addressing disparities in access, the data often reveals disproportionate impacts on specific groups, spanning different ethnicities and socio-economic statuses. Therefore, addressing complex issues requires targeted, nuanced strategies, rather than generalized approaches, in order to foster meaningful change for those most adversely affected.

How To Approach Formulating the Strategy

Strategy: The Focus Area

When engaging in economic mobility initiatives for a community, it is advisable to consider the broader region rather than focusing solely on individual geographic areas. This approach recognizes that economies operate without strict boundaries; city limits do not restrict economic activity, and most individuals are unconcerned with municipal divisions.

For example, in the Atlanta metropolitan area, approximately 70% of workers commute across county lines each day. Businesses similarly interact with clients and supply chains that extend beyond local borders. While public transportation may not be the central focus of this work, it remains an essential factor in promoting equity. Connecting metropolitan regions is vital to ensuring residents can reliably access employment opportunities regardless of their location.

Research conducted by the Atlanta Regional Commission in 2017 highlights the economic benefits of such investments: reducing the average worker's commute time by one hour effectively increases annual salaries by $1,000. If commute times were reduced for even 20 percent of Atlanta's workforce, the regional economy could see an infusion of approximately $460 million.

Regional companies also stand to gain from improved transportation networks, which enhance productivity by providing access to skilled labor across all shifts. Such improvements bolster regional competitiveness and foster a more robust business climate. Ultimately, addressing equity concerns through strategic transportation investment is both ethically sound and economically advantageous.

A regional approach is optimal for strategy development, as it enables consideration of the full context of individuals and families. This perspective offers several key advantages:

- Comprehensive Resource Allocation: Regional strategies allow for more effective distribution of resources, ensuring that support reaches areas with the greatest need.
- Economic Interdependence: Individuals and businesses often operate across municipal boundaries; a regional view captures these economic connections and promotes coordinated growth.
- Transportation and Infrastructure: Addressing issues such as commute times and access to services is more

effective when planned at a regional level, improving overall quality of life.

- Data Driven Decision Making: Regional analysis provides a broader dataset, leading to more informed decisions and targeted interventions.
- Equitable Outcomes: By considering diverse communities within a region, strategies are better positioned to address disparities and promote inclusive economic mobility.

Without this perspective, strategies risk overlooking critical components necessary for effective economic mobility and long-term success.

The Goal: What Does Success Look Like

Establishing shared objectives among all partners is essential to the success of any strategy. Equally important, is to systematically monitor progress throughout the partnership and effort. Program administrators bear the responsibility of evaluating business and organizational outcomes, as successful tracking is crucial for measuring achievements and overall advancement over time. A robust and shared tracking mechanism benefits participants, funders, civil society and organizational stakeholders alike.

Program success should be defined by both immediate and long-term goals. When articulating these objectives, consider the intended audience, appropriate timelines, and necessary steps toward achieving broader aspirations. Regular check-ins help ensure continued relevance for all stakeholders, while comprehensive data monitoring facilitates timely adjustments when needed.

Transparency in reporting metrics is fundamental to organizational integrity and the strategy. Publicly sharing progress, regardless of pace, fosters trust and accountability. The most efficient approach is to make this information accessible online, with a commitment to update results consistently—whether monthly or quarterly. Certain metrics may require more frequent updates than others, but the obligation to provide timely data is owed to the community.

Clear presentation of key metrics is essential. Utilize graphs, charts, notable figures, and visual representations to communicate objectives and progress effectively. These efforts are aimed at enabling the community to comprehend both the organization's goals and its impact.

Achieving genuine equity will require sustained, long-term commitment following generations of disparity. Cities strive to excel in areas such as business environment and entrepreneurship, yet minimizing income inequality remains a vital target. In Atlanta, addressing this issue has been a consistent mission, notwithstanding the challenges and gradual nature of progress. Immediate results are uncommon; instead, deliberate and measured strategies are necessary to achieve significant change.

Each new program should align closely with established objectives, supporting desired outcomes and demonstrating impact. Clear communication regarding each initiative's contribution to overarching goals motivates teams, communities, and stakeholders to continue advancing the work.

Implementing these strategies is complex. Persistent issues, including food and medical deserts and limited retail amenities, present considerable obstacles. While government can incentivize, legislate, and promote development, it cannot compel private sector investment, hiring, or location decisions beyond democratic means. This underscores the importance of forming partnerships and pursuing collaborative solutions to achieve mutually beneficial outcomes that ultimately support the community.

For example, addressing food insecurity is particularly challenging, as grocery retailers tend to favor established markets and assess risk thoroughly before investing in underserved communities. Government can build relationships and advocate for the need, but ultimately, investment decisions rest with private enterprises' internal real estate committees who have no understanding of a particular community if not through a data lens. It is for this reason that progress may not always be visible on the ground, especially where relationship-building is concerned, leading to misconceptions about a lack of the strategy's advancement.

With robust data and clearly defined goals, the organization can effectively articulate results, measure impact, and demonstrate progress. This transparency supports stronger leadership alignment, enables real-time strategic adjustments, and drives continuous improvement across initiatives.

Establish the Rules

Every community can contribute to efforts that can collectively influence broader societal outcomes. Collaborative action can help address longstanding issues of unequal access and opportunity, potentially leading to sustainable change. Such initiatives often begin with conversations among key stakeholders.

At an event recognizing Martin Luther King Jr., attendees discussed challenging topics in facilitated group conversations. As a facilitator, I presented questions provided by organizers, prompting discussions about inequity. One scenario introduced was joining a game of Monopoly after several properties had already been bought, illustrating limitations in ownership opportunities and income generation. This example highlighted how late entry or restricted access can affect participants' ability to accumulate assets and compete on equal terms—an experience paralleled by some individuals facing current economic challenges.

Following the event, it became evident that various community members and business owners may not be aware of critical information such as financial rules, resources, or strategies necessary for economic participation. Factors like understanding ownership, credit scores, capital costs, banking services, financial planning and property ownership play a role in wealth creation. Education, banking, savings, and asset accumulation have been identified as important elements for building family wealth, which supports current and future generations. And yet, many communities do not have access to this type of information.

Therefore, strategies to address income inequality must ensure equitable access to the knowledge and resources required for economic engagement, as these are the foundational standards for inclusion in society. When all families have access and knowledge of these tools, broader and sustained participation in long-term economic inclusion becomes possible.

Implementation Framework

At the core, the implementation framework needs to be nimble to adapt to the changing times, focused on eliminating the years of inequities found throughout current policy frameworks and adapted to each community.

The nation continues to face issues of inequality and unequal access to basic community amenities and economic opportunities. The growth in inequality is attributable to a combination of factors, including various government policies and programs established over many years. While it is not suggested that all policymakers intended negative outcomes, these accumulated policies have contributed to inequity in communities across the United States. Addressing these disparities and years of disinvestment requires focused leadership and sustained effort.

Current economic and community development challenges are the result of long-term trends, and solutions cannot be expected to resolve them immediately. For the greatest impact, equitable strategies must be implemented incrementally, building on previous efforts towards more inclusive outcomes. Inequality has developed over time and is embedded within existing policy structures; therefore, creating an equitable environment will require ongoing work across multiple years.

The pursuit of equity is a continuous process, and opening a dialogue now lays the foundation for future progress. This responsibility spans generations, emphasizing the importance of establishing a pathway toward greater fairness at every opportunity. Collaborative planning and strategy development are necessary to achieve meaningful change at the community level. Effective strategies should allow for rebuilding, adjustment, and innovation, adapting to present and future needs.

A flexible approach to strategy is essential; strategies must be able to evolve alongside shifts in the economy to maximize their impact. As noted by Bill Gates, adaptation is key for effective outcomes in changing conditions.

This proposed strategy serves as a framework to address inequality, intended for adaptation by individual communities according to their unique needs and circumstances. Communities should select relevant elements based on factors such as politics, policy, budget, timing, impact, relevance, and community feedback. Consensus among stakeholders is important in formulating and implementing these approaches.

An Equity Strategy Focus

When considering an equity strategy, there are many ways the government can have a direct impact on the success and impact of the overall strategy; I will highlight the 4 focus areas I feel are essential when considering this work.

First, each program should establish opportunities for individuals to develop their most applicable skill sets. Providing accessible information about available training programs supports increased success. These pathways may include formal education (such as grammar school, high school, or college), skills training (technical schools), or on-the-job and apprenticeship learning. Recognizing that individuals learn in diverse ways, it is important to offer adaptable learning opportunities to support successful outcomes in equity-focused programming. The fundamental objective is to help people acquire the skills necessary to earn a livable wage (with further detail found in the Role of Data section).

Second, the strategy needs to focus on all levels of community inclusion. Community meetings often reveal that residents dedicate time and effort to participate, which demonstrates their engagement with their locality and desire to contribute. At a meeting in Atlanta discussing neighborhood empowerment, one resident explained her interest in being included in local investment and development processes, so that changes occur collaboratively rather than unilaterally. Other attendees generally agreed with this perspective, emphasizing an interest in participating in development projects for reasons related to community identity, economic opportunity, and self-determination. On the other hand, when residents are not taken into consideration it can be frustrating for them as they possess unique knowledge of their community's history and culture, which ultimately can benefit new investments and ongoing development.

Cities need to remember that people make choices about where they want to live. In the advent of remote work, moving has become a reality for many families and they are choosing inclusive cities. Consequently, establishing a meaningful and distinctive "quality of place" benefits all community members. A well-developed inclusive strategy can facilitate this process.

Dr. Michael Porter of Harvard Business School has stated that strategy involves making choices and distinguishing oneself. What has transpired is that people want to be part of cities where policies and programs promote broadly shared growth and success. In other words, cities that value their history, utilize present assets, and prepare their constituents for the future are where today's workforce want to live.

Third, a competitive city seeks to integrate equity into their pursuit of jobs, investment, and small business development. This requires a clear strategy and collaborative approach to implementing equitable policies and programs. While the government is not the sole agent in fostering these types of investments, they can play a significant role when community involvement is prioritized. Direct experience with economic development programs in underinvested neighborhoods illustrates that purposeful government-led initiatives can influence positive outcomes by the private corporations and small businesses.

For example, in one community lacking full-service financial institutions and served mainly by payday lenders, the Federal Reserve's 2017 *Survey of Household Economics and Decision Making* found that 20% of Black and Hispanic low-income households (earning less than $40,000 annually) did not have a bank account, compared with only 1% of families earning above $40,000. In this case, it means unbanked families are relying on short-term lending to manage their financing. The challenge with this sort of financial option is the cost to the family. These short-term lending businesses charge annual interest that can reach upwards of 450%.[29] There is no question that this type of financing makes a family's ability to build wealth very difficult, if not impossible. In this case, government policies can change the trajectory for the community. More about what was done in this specific case will come under Partnerships.

Entrepreneurship is another programming approach that can help promote equity in communities. Small businesses offer amenities that contribute to the overall quality of a city and its vibrancy. Business owners support themselves and their families, and these enterprises are sometimes passed on to the next generation, potentially generating wealth for both the present and future. This accumulation of wealth can benefit families economically and may also impact the community by providing local employment opportunities and services. Entrepreneurs play a role in developing local business ecosystems. The Los Angeles Times conducted a survey and found that minority business owners tend to hire minority workers[30]. And in fact, the Joint Center for Political and Economic Studies found that the minority business owners will recruit minority workers from low-income neighborhoods, participate in targeted youth programs and welfare recipients at a higher rate than other business owners.[31] Hence, entrepreneurship is a key strategy when formulating a path to equitable programming in any city.

Fourth, government should prioritize affordable housing as a central component of the equity strategy. According to the United States Department of Housing and Urban Development, individuals spending more than 30% of their income on housing are considered cost burdened. In 2025, the National Housing Conference reported that 53 cities had median rents exceeding this threshold, indicating widespread affordability challenges for renters.[32] The situation is similarly difficult for homebuyers, with over 45% of major metropolitan areas now requiring a six-figure income to purchase a home. This trend is not isolated; housing affordability has declined across nearly all major U.S. metro areas over the past five years.[33] Addressing the housing crisis will require a comprehensive approach—there is no single solution, and a variety of programs and strategies must be considered to make meaningful progress.

An equity strategy that incorporates all four of the following critical focus areas offers the greatest potential for success:

1. **Skill Set Development:** Empowering individuals with relevant education and training to enhance economic mobility.

2. **Community Inclusion:** Ensuring all voices are represented and engaged in decision-making processes.

3. **Jobs, Investment, and Small Business Development:** Promoting job creation, attracting investment, and supporting entrepreneurship to drive economic growth.

4. **Affordable Housing:** Providing access to housing that is financially sustainable for individuals and families.

Integrating these elements creates a comprehensive framework for advancing equity and achieving meaningful, long-term community impact.

While other focus areas are important, an equity strategy that does not include these four critical elements—skill set development, community inclusion, jobs and small business development, and affordable housing—is unlikely to succeed. By focusing on these areas and targeting communities with the greatest need, organizations can maximize their impact.

Drawing on practical experience, this book acknowledges the gap between theory and real-world implementation, and addresses the realities of budgetary, temporal, and staffing constraints. Balancing immediate needs with evidence-based outcomes is essential. The following sections will further examine each focus area within the context of a community's equity strategy.

Equity at Scale Model

A New Model

Identifying programs with measurable impact is central to advancing equity within communities. Achieving this requires implementing a new, outcomes-focused model of service delivery for all those on the ground doing this work. The need for this approach became evident during a presentation on affordable housing initiatives—including down payment assistance, real estate tax freeze programs, and owner-occupied rehabilitation. While the presentation clearly outlined program criteria, access procedures and impact, a participant's question during the discussion - "Why are you presenting compartmentalized solutions when we do not live compartmentalized lives?" - prompted significant personal reflection and has led to the basis of this theory.

This insight highlights the importance of designing programs that address the interconnected needs of individuals —such as education, childcare, banking, retail access, nutritious food, and employment opportunities—rather than focusing solely on isolated solutions like affordable housing. While affordable housing is essential, it cannot be the sole focus of an effective strategy; no single area alone is sufficient to drive meaningful change within a community. The ultimate goal is to develop integrated initiatives that enhance quality of life and foster stronger, more resilient communities, enabling individuals to pursue their aspirations.

The perspective shared by this community member fundamentally reshaped both my personal outlook and the organization's approach to economic and community development growth initiatives. This pivotal moment prompted a transition from isolated programs to a more integrated, holistic ecosystem of services. Achieving sustainable change requires addressing interconnected needs—such as employment, food security, mental health, substance use, education and childcare—rather than treating these issues in isolation. While previous strategies may have focused on specific areas due to funding, capacity, or organizational interests, it is now clear that collaborative efforts are essential for meaningful impact. This new model envisions structures where either a single organization or a coalition of partners can deliver interconnected services. Recognizing that every community is unique, the most effective model should be determined by those within the community who are committed to this work.

The first model to consider when leading this work is a single-organization-coordinator approach. In Atlanta, for example, Westside Works operates one of the region's most successful job placement programs, achieving over 90% job placement rates on the stadium project for participants completing training. A key factor in their success is dedicated advocacy: the team ensures each participant attends training and promptly addresses barriers—such as transportation, childcare, or personal challenges—that might impede progress. This immediate support helps participants quickly reengage. The participant, in turn, also works closely with Westside Future Fund, another non-profit in the community, who focuses on building single-family and rental affordable housing, promoting financial literacy, and fostering community engagement. By integrating multiple initiatives under one roof, the organization delivers more effective and targeted community support. Their success has inspired other communities to consider establishing a "community quarterback" to coordinate equity-focused efforts.

In a second model in which a coalition of partners provide interconnected services delivery, program leaders must think expansively and innovatively to maximize positive outcomes. This does not necessitate providing all services independently; rather, it calls for building collaborative networks with partners whose missions align. Understanding when to lead, collaborate, or support others amplifies collective impact.

In either model, the strategy should adopt a people-centric ecosystem that uplifts entire communities comprehensively. Redevelopment typically involves agencies with distinct yet complementary focuses—such as workforce development, housing, transportation, and economic development—each contributing specialized expertise to the broader effort. To maximize impact, organizations must move beyond conventional thinking and coordinate their efforts through intentional collaboration and integration. By sharing key performance indicators and aligning objectives, metrics, and target groups, these entities can leverage their collective strengths for the greater community good.

Admittedly, this approach may present challenges. Organizational resources and staffing structures are often deeply tied to institutional survival, making consolidation or restructuring complex. Aligning diverse missions may be complicated by culture, funding streams or even institutional investors. Nevertheless, because resources will always be finite, a people-centric model seeks to optimize existing assets for broader community benefit. Success demands leveraging organizational expertise, available funding, team commitment, and shared mission focus. Further discussion on fostering collaboration for community advancement appears in the Partnerships section of this book.

At its core, equity requires meeting individuals and businesses where they are, equipping them with tailored supports necessary for positive outcomes. Ideally, all empowerment programs should align directly with the needs and circumstances of those served. As illustrated below, such a delivery model would offer a cohesive and impactful framework for community support.

In other words, a truly equitable approach recognizes that barriers to opportunity are often unique and multifaceted. Individuals and businesses may face challenges related to language, transportation, access to capital, education, or systemic discrimination. By designing programs that are flexible and responsive to these diverse realities, organizations and service providers can ensure that support is not only available but also accessible and relevant. A tailored, people-centered model also fosters trust and engagement within the community. When individuals see that programs are designed with their specific needs in mind—whether that means offering services in multiple languages, providing flexible hours, or integrating wraparound supports such as childcare, education and financial counseling—they are more likely to participate and benefit. This, in turn, leads to stronger outcomes and more sustainable progress.

Moreover, aligning empowerment programs with the lived experiences of those served enables organizations and service providers to measure impact more effectively. By setting clear, individualized goals and tracking progress, organizations can adapt strategies in real time, ensuring resources are used efficiently and outcomes are maximized.

Ultimately, a cohesive, individual-centric framework not only advances equity but also strengthens the social and economic fabric of the entire community. It creates an environment where all members—regardless of background or circumstance—have the opportunity to thrive and contribute to collective community success.

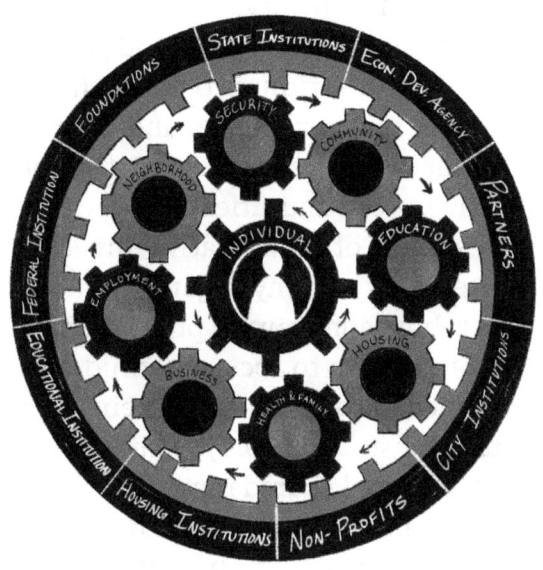

Figure 2.2 An individual centric framework [34]

As is illustrated above, governments, service providers, and nonprofits should design tailored programs that address individual needs, representing an optimal approach for supporting diverse communities globally. This strategy emphasizes an individual-centric model, where essential services—such as education, business support, housing, and employment—form the immediate circle around an individual. Partners who facilitate access to these services comprise the outer circle, creating a network of support that adapts to changing circumstances.

The conceptual framework can be visualized as interconnected gears, illustrating how personal situations or shifting priorities may alter service requirements. For example, if an individual is unable to secure employment, their focus may shift toward training opportunities, which can improve job prospects and better align with their lifestyle. The model is designed to be nimble, adjusting to economic forces and personal situations as needed. Similarly, organizations providing these services may change over time, but the core needs and focus areas remain consistent. This adaptability ensures that the model remains relevant and effective as communities evolve.

A practical example of collaborative impact is the partnership between United Way and my organization, Invest Atlanta. United Way offers robust community programming and utilizes a Child Wealth Score metric to focus on child well-being. Both organizations recognized that child well-being is closely linked to parents maintaining stable employment and housing. To ensure alignment, we adopted shared metrics for tracking success, fostering mutual accountability. This partnership secured funding for a business grant program and enhanced visibility into businesses supported through joint efforts. While initial outcomes have been positive, ongoing analysis of metrics and long-term impact will provide further insights into the effectiveness of this collaborative approach.

While recognizing the merits of this strategy, it is important to acknowledge challenges at the community implementation level and in sustaining long-term outcomes for individuals and communities. Direct delivery models can be complex and financially demanding, particularly for smaller governments or organizations seeking ongoing involvement. For example, one entrepreneur may require specialized accounting support, while another might need commercial security solutions—necessitating distinct programs and resources for each. Funding and administrative capacity must also expand to support both service delivery and organizational infrastructure. Although managing two bespoke initiatives may be feasible, scaling such an individualized approach to thousands of community members and small business presents substantial efficiency and effectiveness challenges, raising concerns about its long-term sustainability.

While direct engagement with individuals and businesses remains vital—and is deeply fulfilling for many professionals in this sector—the fundamental goal should be to implement empowering, equity-based programs that deliver measurable impact, remain cost-effective, and foster equity across entire communities. Without such scalable and sustainable models, the risk is that meaningful progress will not be achieved. Therefore, finding a balanced approach that aligns resources and capacity with community needs is essential for the success of any equity strategy.

The Equity at Scale Model Explained

The persistent challenge lies in the fact that many communities have seen little fundamental change over time. Reflecting on Martin Luther King's *The American Dream* sermon, delivered on July 4, 1965, it becomes clear that numerous neighborhoods continue to grapple with longstanding issues. These challenges include limited retail options, inadequate access to healthy food, low performing schools, a lack of medical services, insufficient low-cost transportation, and constrained banking resources. Concerns also persist regarding the safety of families within these environments.

While significant efforts have been made to address such issues, driving and sustaining systemic change remains an arduous process, leaving many communities vulnerable. Traditional models often struggle to adapt to the evolving dynamics of these environments. Within a capitalist framework, the United States experiences economic fluctuations as a natural consequence of its market structure. During these periods of economic decline, what the data presents is disproportionately affects in underinvested neighborhoods, exacerbating their existing vulnerabilities.

As previously discussed, programmatic interventions must focus on an individual's needs; in this respect, it is imperative to broaden this perspective to encompass both individuals and the contexts in which they live within the person-centric model. In the model, there is an acknowledgment that each person's situation may differ from broader community circumstances. Hence, for maximal impact within the equity framework, strategies must intersect community-wide needs with those of individuals.

If a community possesses sufficient resources, the first person-centric model is ideal in driving impact. Conversely, where financial resources and partner capacity are limited and broad-based equitable initiatives are necessary for sustainable transformation, the On Demand Empowerment Ecosystem approach offers an alternative within the Equity at Scale Model (EaS), to bring about an equitable, scalable and lasting impact to community.

The On Demand Empowerment Ecosystem

Rather than emphasizing theoretical constructs, the EaS Model is designed for practical and meaningful outcomes while recognizing local economic and capacity constraints. By centering equity, EaS seeks an innovative service delivery method to generate durable benefits, expanding pathways out of poverty while recognizing resource (financial and personal) limitations faced by implementing organizations.

The graph below depicts the On Demand Empowerment Ecosystem (ODE). The ODE empowers individuals to access services 'on demand' when, where, and how they need them, offering a flexible menu of options tailored to diverse circumstances. By balancing limited resources with the pursuit of equity, this model reframes service delivery to emphasize accessibility, equality and economic mobility.

A key feature of ODE is its reliance on partnerships among mission-aligned organizations, rather than requiring a single entity to deliver all services. This collaborative ecosystem enables partners to collectively provide the breadth of support necessary for individuals to achieve economic advancement, while also sharing responsibility for resource allocation. Such an approach fosters innovation, leverages specialized expertise, and ensures that services remain responsive to evolving community needs.

Long-term sustainability is essential for the success of ODE. Early attention to resource distribution helps establish a foundation for enduring impact. The "On Demand Empowerment" ecosystem within the EaS framework recognizes that specific services will vary according to local context, and that adaptability is crucial. Both community and partner engagement are vital for identifying, refining, and delivering the services required to support economic mobility.

Ultimately, ODE offers a scalable, resilient blueprint that can be tailored to the unique needs of any community, ensuring equitable access and fostering lasting progress in the equity strategy through an On Demand Empowerment Ecosystem.

On-Demand Empowerment Menu

Figure 2.3 On Demand Empowerment

The accompanying graph provides a clear visualization of the On Demand Empowerment (ODE) ecosystem as conceptualized within the Equity at Scale (EaS) Model. Several key features are highlighted:

1) Community-Centric Focus: The Equity at Scale (EaS) Model prioritizes the collective needs of the broader community, encouraging individuals to collaborate, learn, and grow together. This approach fosters shared progress and supports the advancement of all members within the community.

2) Individual Empowerment: Within this framework, every individual is empowered to select services tailored to their unique circumstances from a diverse range of providers. Opportunities are presented as structured packages or can be self-determined, ensuring that support is both relevant and accessible. By placing choice and agency in the hands of individuals, the model enhances engagement and satisfaction, while simultaneously increasing the capacity of service providers to deliver efficient and impactful support to those who need it most.

3) Equitable Access to Service Providers: A cornerstone of the On Demand Empowerment (ODE) ecosystem is the guarantee of equal access to designated resources for every community member. This commitment to equity ensures that no service is out of reach and that all individuals have the tools necessary to achieve positive outcomes. Barriers to access are systematically minimized, reinforcing fairness and inclusion at the heart of the EaS Model.

4) Diverse Service Offerings: The model intentionally differentiates its array of services to maximize opportunities for each individual to pursue their goals. This diversity ensures that a wide spectrum of needs and aspirations can be addressed,

empowering all community members to access resources most relevant to their circumstances. By offering a variety of tailored supports, the EaS Model cultivates an environment where everyone is equipped to thrive. Importantly, the system recognizes that needs may change over time, allowing individuals and communities to return whenever new challenges or opportunities arise

5) Engage: Once an individual or community chooses their path —whether a single service or a suite of opportunities—the true journey begins with engagement. Success is not a fixed destination, but a dynamic pathway that may bend and evolve over time. Each step forward, no matter how winding, is a testament to resilience and growth. By embracing new opportunities and remaining committed to progress, both individuals and communities can transform aspirations into achievement. The pursuit of success is ongoing, and every act of engagement strengthens the foundation for a brighter, more equitable future.

The subsequent section of this book will delve deeper into the EaS Model, breaking down each component in detail to provide a comprehensive guide for the successful execution of equity-focused work.

The When

Time constraints pose significant challenges for individuals managing work, educational, familial, and personal commitments. This underscores the critical importance of timing in the effectiveness of ODE.

Traditional government and nonprofit service delivery programs typically operate from 9:00 a.m. to 5:00 p.m., Monday through Friday. While this structure is suitable for an organization's operations, it probably does not adequately address the needs of community members with parallel obligations. In response to evolving work patterns, particularly since the onset of COVID-19, there has been increased demand for flexible scheduling. Accordingly, government and nonprofit programs must adapt by providing around-the-clock accessibility. For this reason, this component of the EaS model is designated as On Demand Empowerment (ODE), ensuring continuous access.

When developing an ODE ecosystem, organizations can consider multiple options to enhance accessibility and responsiveness. One approach involves adjusting physical office hours, such as offering later openings and closings during the week or shifting schedules to provide Saturday hours. This flexibility benefits both employees and the public by enabling evening and weekend services.

However, ODE distinguishes itself by expanding beyond variable office hours to include comprehensive online access to all programs. Leveraging technology, the online portal provides individuals with a range of tools available 24/7, including instructional videos, service request forms, and artificial intelligence support for immediate assistance. This digital infrastructure ensures that constituents can engage with services at their convenience, overcoming traditional barriers related to time and location.

By integrating both flexible in-person options and robust online resources, the ODE ecosystem creates a more inclusive and adaptable service delivery model. This approach not only meets individuals where they are but also empowers them to access the support they need, when and how they need it, driving greater equity and economic mobility within the community

The Where

The landscape of government and nonprofit service delivery is undergoing significant transformation. Traditional models—requiring individuals to travel through congested city traffic and secure parking at centralized offices—are rapidly becoming obsolete. Within the On Demand Empowerment (ODE) ecosystem, organizations are now expected to proactively enhance accessibility for in-person engagement.

One effective approach involves distributing physical service locations throughout the communities served. This enables individuals to manage essential tasks more efficiently, such as visiting a government office after dropping off a child at school or before heading to work. Enhanced proximity increases the likelihood that services reach their intended recipients and ensures essential programs are more attainable.

Importantly, improved accessibility does not require dedicated standalone office buildings, which can present financial challenges for smaller entities. Strategic placement in commonly frequented venues—such as shared workspaces, recreation centers, or grocery stores—can be both practical and cost-effective. Collaborative partnerships with organizations that share similar objectives can yield mutual benefits for communities and entrepreneurs seeking support and resources.

For example, Invest Atlanta has achieved notable success by co-locating with both public and private partner organizations focused on business development. These arrangements have, in some instances, resulted in reduced rental costs in exchange for providing dedicated office hours to workspace members. Such mutually advantageous relationships reinforce the ODE model's commitment to equitable access.

To further this mission, Invest Atlanta launched a hub-style office at the Russell Center of Innovation along their Financial Access corridor. Here, the small business loan team provides real-time consulting to all visitors and businesses, ensuring ongoing, accessible support for the community. Establishing these types of collaborative relationships is essential for increasing accessibility and empowering individuals to succeed within the broader equity strategy. By embedding services within trusted community spaces and fostering partnerships, organizations can more effectively reach those who need support, adapt to evolving needs, and drive meaningful, sustainable impact.

The How

As each new generation reaches maturity, they introduce innovative engagement practices, most notably the adoption of social media platforms for peer communication and service discovery. Recognizing these shifts, it is critical within the ODE ecosystem model for organizations to adapt and facilitate emerging methods of communication.

A central tenet of the ODE model is establishing numerous access points. These may include virtual office hours, YouTube programming featuring pre-recorded business seminars accessible across major social media platforms (such as X, LinkedIn, Facebook, Instagram, and WhatsApp), and, notably, an online chat function. To remain connected with businesses assisted by our organization, I proactively visit them and routinely discover needs for improved support channels. For example, upon learning that entrepreneurs sometimes abandon applications due to unanswered questions, we launched an online chat function monitored by a dedicated team member. This resource, available during business hours, offers real-time support, with responses averaging eight seconds and earning a 4.8 service rating—an initiative with minimal investment but significant impact on accessibility.

Social media platforms have become indispensable tools for community engagement and are now expected features in providing continuous service to businesses. While it can be challenging to manage multiple platforms, leveraging more than one allows organizations to meet individuals according to their preferences, aligning with ODE's goal of ensuring broad access.

The advent of AI and bot technology has significantly reduced the costs of maintaining a robust social media presence, making these solutions increasingly viable for all communities. While technology cannot fully address every inquiry or replace human interaction, it efficiently handles initial contact, allowing staff to focus on complex and specialized matters.

The ODE ecosystem model is designed to meet constituents where they are—a fundamental aspect of modern service delivery. Adoption of these technologies and strategies necessitates organizational investment in both personnel and infrastructure to create environments that foster access for businesses and communities.

Crucially, the "how" of the ODE model prioritizes real-time feedback and superior customer service. Although some entities and government agencies may not consistently excel in this area, prompt responses and available support markedly improve client experiences, especially when navigating complex program offerings.

Implementing such programs can be resource-intensive, primarily due to staffing requirements, but leveraging social media enhances the sustainability of the ODE platform. The success of online resource programs underscores the value of always-available support staff. Stakeholders appreciated both the assistance provided and the genuine responsiveness to their needs, justifying the long-term investment.

One key insight from this experience was the benefit of immediate, real-time feedback, which enables rapid issue identification before escalation and improves service quality. Maintaining open communication loops is also essential for sustaining positive relationships with boards, executive committees, or elected officials—critical influencers whose support underpins organizational longevity.

For example, when tasked with distributing $15 million through a business grant program, external contractors were engaged to expedite fund disbursement. However, when their contracts ended, oversight of follow-up inquiries lapsed, resulting in temporary communication breakdowns. Fortunately, the online chat function served as a crucial fallback, allowing messages to be promptly addressed once the issue was identified. This experience underscores the importance of implementing circular or redundant communication methods to enhance service delivery and prevent avoidable errors. By establishing multiple channels for stakeholder engagement and feedback, organizations can ensure continuity, responsiveness, and higher levels of satisfaction among those they serve.

Today, as individuals thoughtfully select where to live, work, and raise families, cities bear responsibility for attracting and retaining residents. Building vibrant communities is a collaborative effort, and both the community and the ODE platform have integral roles to play in this ongoing process.

The Who

No single organization can provide all necessary services to every individual. The key to effective collaboration lies in recognizing when to lead, when to follow, and when to offer support. Each of these roles is essential to achieving the desired outcomes, yet it is typically unrealistic for any one provider to fulfill all functions that is unless they are very well capitalized. Consequently, it is critical to engage in discussions that identify which entity is best positioned to deliver specific services, as this dialogue is fundamental to advancing overall equity efforts. The formation of these relationships will be further detailed in the Partnerships section. For now, it is important to note that a thorough understanding of the service provider landscape is a vital starting point.

Such discussions with partners may present challenges, as they can affect funding streams, jurisdictional boundaries, and potentially the existence of some organizations. Nevertheless, these conversations are indispensable for ensuring equity in program delivery. It is advisable to prioritize the needs of the end user throughout these deliberations. The central consideration should not be which agency will implement a program, but rather which is most suitably equipped to deliver the required type of service. This aspect will be explored in greater depth within the ODE model discussion on Partnerships.

Regarding sustainability, advancing equity requires long-term commitment. Partners must maintain openness and transparency concerning the ongoing costs associated with service provision under the ODE ecosystem model. Failure to account for these expenses from the outset may jeopardize the partnership and hinder progress. Collaborative approaches to identifying funding sources will benefit the entire initiative.

The Which

For optimal results in any program, it is important to provide a broad selection of offerings across multiple delivery platforms, including online, social, and in-person options. This ensures that information about available loans, grants, programs, and services is accessible through various engagement points, allowing the community to obtain necessary resources efficiently. While centralizing resources into a single, user-friendly platform is not a new idea, it remains valuable for improving navigation and access as the platform can be tailored by language and other disability friendly features.

An example of this approach is the development of a Business Portal accessible in person, via social media, or online. Such a portal consolidates information on grants, loans, licenses, and other entrepreneurial resources, as well as partner organization services like technical assistance, training, and hiring support. The objective is to make all channels effective entry points for information access.

To enhance accessibility, programming details should be organized into a user-friendly toolkit structured in individual services or packages. Complex portals can result in user confusion and hinder engagement. Incorporating a feedback mechanism, such as a website survey tool, enables ongoing improvements by collecting user input. For instance, the implementation of a survey tool for a grant program provided actionable insights, informing subsequent program designs and streamlining document submission processes. Feedback from users indicated challenges with repeated documentation requests due to delays; adjustments were made in future programs to minimize redundant requests and request key information closer to project initiation. Ongoing feedback supports continuous evaluation and adaptation to meet the evolving needs of service recipients, ensuring relevance and effectiveness in delivering resources and support.

While consolidating resources into a single, user-friendly

toolkit is valuable, it is essential to address potential content overload and ensure ease of use. Simply compiling information is not enough—if users cannot easily find what they need, or if the volume of content becomes overwhelming, the toolkit loses its effectiveness. To maximize value, it is advisable to engage a skilled marketing team to tailor messaging and organize tools in a functional, intuitive manner. This approach ensures that all programs and resources are easily discoverable and accessible to the intended audience.

Five Criteria to Offering Business Support

Similar to working with individuals, equity initiatives for business requires meeting businesses where they are. This necessitates adapting technical assistance to the time, location, and way businesses seek guidance. Accordingly, effective technical assistance programs should adhere to five primary criteria to support businesses in their development:

1) Provide multiple access points, both physical and digital.
2) Ensure availability at various times, recognizing that many entrepreneurs cannot leave their operations during standard business hours; therefore, offering after-hours and weekend support is essential.
3) Deliver services through online and in-person formats and maintain an accessible library of resources for entrepreneurs.
4) Incorporate both structured cohort participation and individualized options, as businesses may prefer different forms of engagement.
5) Offer a comprehensive suite of services to address the evolving needs of businesses at different stages.

By delivering a broad array of technical assistance offerings, organizations can effectively respond to the unique challenges businesses face throughout their journey. The success of businesses contributes directly to the growth of families, neighborhood jobs, communities, and the enterprises themselves.

The importance of technical assistance is well-documented. For instance, SBA's reported that those businesses in one of their technical assistance programs saw a 60% bid win rate and a 45% increase in annual revenue.[35] More significantly, the research demonstrated that technical assistance not only facilitated business initiation and growth but also enhanced recipients' ability to secure future funding or become more appealing to commercial banks and investors.

Although projecting the long-term outcomes of such interventions is challenging, available evidence suggests that technical assistance forms a solid foundation for business success. Specifically, technical assistance can support businesses in the following ways:

- Improve Business and Financial Preparation: Helps small businesses develop best in class business, financial, legal, marketing, and management plans, and establish proper accounting systems.
- Increase Access to Different Capital Sources: Assists businesses in presenting themselves more professionally to lenders, making it easier to secure loans for growth and expansion.
- Enhance Revenue: Identify strategies that can grow revenue opportunities.
- Improve Contract Performance: Increase knowledge of the bidding process.
- Disaster Recovery: Creating plans that allow for the business to prepare of financial and natural disasters.

In summary, businesses with robust accounting, financial management, marketing strategies, and legal frameworks are better positioned to achieve their objectives.

For example, an entrepreneur expressed appreciation for our support after participating in the CAREs Act program, which included both a grant and access to technical assistance. Although initially uninterested in the technical component, she later recognized that the guidance—particularly in establishing an online presence—provided enduring benefits that far exceeded the short-term impact of the grant funds. By developing a strong online presence, she increased her sales by 30% and was able to hire additional staff for her flower shop.

It is also crucial to design technical assistance programs that address the distinct needs of Black, Hispanic and other targeted entrepreneurs. Such programs must consider both foundational business acumen and the specific ways race and ethnicity influence access to resources, financing, and community relationships. For instance, a Milken Institute study identified low credit scores as the leading reason for capital denials among some of these groups.[36] However, factors such as cultural barriers, generational poverty, educational attainment, professional development, immigration status, experiences of discrimination, and trust must also be addressed to strengthen these enterprises. Technical assistance tailored to these realities can play a pivotal role in revitalizing underinvested neighborhoods within our communities.

Operation Hope, led by John Hope Bryant, has conducted research on credit scores. Bryant developed the Community Credit Score Index, which tracks average credit scores in neighborhoods and incorporates factors such as education, homeownership, income, life expectancy, and crime. The findings indicate a clear difference in economic conditions between neighborhoods with lower and higher credit scores. Lower credit score communities tend to have more check cashers, liquor stores, and payday lenders, while higher credit score areas typically feature more banks and retail establishments. The objective of the index is to ensure community members and entrepreneurs understand the impact of credit scores on their personal and business' finances.[37]

Understanding the impact on credit scores and increasing the likelihood of business success can be advanced by integrating technical assistance programming with an understanding of many financing options. This approach has the potential to produce significant positive outcomes. While many businesses prefer grants, the current economic environment makes grants difficult to maintain at all levels of government—federal, state, county, and city. A revolving loan fund, however, can provide favorable terms and serve as an effective option for communities seeking sustainable solutions. Collaborating with mission-aligned partners, such as Community Development Financial Institutions, foundations, or non-profit organizations, can enhance the availability of financial support for the business.

Through interactions with numerous businesses and organizations, it is evident that executives may sometimes become highly focused on specific goals, which can detract from attention to broader frameworks necessary for long-term success. For many businesses, especially those led by minorities, access to financial resources remains a significant challenge. However, establishing a strong network of support and technical assistance is equally important. Technical support in areas such as online sales, accounting controls, procurement policies, legal structure, human resources, and cybersecurity greatly contributes to a business's sustainability and growth.

While business owners may possess expertise in their respective trades, additional skills—such as management and accounting—are essential for long-term success. Family-run businesses often benefit when each member contributes unique strengths, helping to ensure overall operational stability.

Accessible entrepreneurial programs are crucial for the long-term viability of small business owners. These initiatives provide a solid foundation for family empowerment, generate measurable financial benefits, and contribute to the creation of local employment opportunities as well as the availability of essential community services.

Metrics

Defining Key Metrics

It is imperative to clearly define even the most commonly used terms and key metrics to ensure that all stakeholders share a unified vision of success within the EaS model. Rather than simply referencing dictionary definitions, this process requires collaborative engagement with the community to both establish and reevaluate terminology. Such an approach is vital for program alignment and is especially crucial for data leaders.

For instance, consider the metric of a "job." While it may seem straightforward, there are important nuances. At Invest Atlanta, we initially tracked jobs solely as net new opportunities for the city. Our methodology has since evolved to distinguish between "middle wage jobs" ($40k–$80k), "good jobs" ($80k+) and "retained jobs", each requiring full-time employment and benefits, among other criteria. Establishing rigorous and universally understood metrics is fundamental; discrepancies in definitions across teams can lead to significant risks for inaccurate reporting.

Post-pandemic, tracking jobs has become increasingly complex. Organizations now need to collect employee ZIP codes for new hires to accurately assess local or regional employment impact. The rise of remote work introduces additional challenges, such as determining whether to include positions located outside the city or country. This also raises considerations around tax jurisdictions, workforce composition by location, housing needs and salary distributions for non-local vs local employees. Maintaining national competitiveness while upholding accountability requires addressing these questions, as they help clarify the true local impact of employment initiatives when working with private industry.

Another important consideration is determining when to report the creation of a housing unit or the job—whether at the time of announcement, agreement signing, or project completion. There is no single correct answer; what matters most is ensuring alignment so that, when metrics are combined, they are compatible and accurately reflect outcomes.

This scenario highlights the critical importance of establishing clear and precise metric definitions within the Equity at Scale (EaS) model. During an annual audit, a consulting firm newly operating in the city was found to have a business practice that, while common in its industry, exposed a significant gap in our program's original metric definitions. Specifically, the company routinely hired and terminated the same employees' multiple times within a single year, each time reporting the rehire as a "new job." This practice was tied to their operational model: as the firm acquired new clients, employees were reassigned from one account to another. For administrative purposes, this transition was processed as a layoff from one account and a rehire onto another, resulting in multiple employment records for the same individual within a short timeframe. From the employee's perspective, these transitions were seamless and did not disrupt their actual employment status. However, in the company's reporting—and consequently in our program's data—each rehire was counted as a distinct "new job."

Although this approach was both legally and corporately permissible, it did not align with the intended outcomes of our incentive programs. The root cause was a lack of specificity in our original definition of what constituted a "new job," particularly regarding employment duration and continuity. As a result, the program's metrics inadvertently overstated the true impact on job creation, undermining the integrity of our reporting and the effectiveness of our incentive structure.

Recognizing the diversity of business models and employment practices across industries, we undertook a comprehensive review and refinement of our metric definitions. The revised definition of a "new job" now explicitly incorporates critical factors such as:

- **Location:** The physical or operational site where the job is based.
- **Benefits:** The provision of health insurance, retirement plans, and other employee benefits.
- **Salary:** The wage or salary level associated with the position.
- **Training Provisions:** Requirements for onboarding, skills development, or certification.

- **Length of Employment:** Minimum duration of continuous employment required for a position to qualify as a "new job" under the program.

By introducing these more rigorous and transparent criteria, we ensure that reported outcomes accurately reflect genuine job creation and align with the broader goals of the EaS model. This experience underscores the necessity for ongoing evaluation and adaptation of program metrics to maintain accountability, foster equitable outcomes, and support sustainable community impact.

Challenging Metrics

Extensive research underscores the critical importance of establishing clear, well-defined goals and metrics within and among organizations. For the successful deployment of the Equity at Scale (EaS) model, it is essential that organizations set annual objectives that are thoughtfully tailored to their available financial and human resources. This targeted approach ensures that strategic initiatives remain both realistic and actionable, maximizing the likelihood of meaningful progress.

In addition to operational metrics, the incorporation of aspirational metrics is invaluable. Aspirational metrics serve as guiding benchmarks that inspire organizations to pursue transformative outcomes beyond immediate operational targets. While the pursuit of both operational and aspirational goals can be complicated by political and environmental factors, their alignment is crucial for fulfilling the organization's mission and driving the effective implementation of the EaS model.

By balancing immediate, resource-based objectives with long-term aspirational targets, organizations are better equipped to address current challenges while maintaining momentum toward their strategic vision. This dual focus fosters a culture of continuous improvement, adaptability, and resilience, enabling organizations to respond proactively to changing circumstances and stakeholder needs. Ultimately, the alignment of operational and aspirational metrics supports sustained progress and ensures that equity-driven initiatives remain impactful over time.

When establishing metrics for organizational performance and program impact, it is often advantageous to define these measures over a multi-year period—such as three years—rather than limiting them to a single fiscal cycle. This approach recognizes the inherent unpredictability of factors such as economic conditions, fundraising capabilities, budget allocations, and shifting political environments. By extending the timeframe for key metrics, organizations can better accommodate unforeseen fluctuations and external disruptions, ensuring that short-term volatility does not derail long-term objectives.

A multi-year perspective also enables organizations to track progress more accurately, identify trends, and make informed adjustments as needed. This strategic flexibility helps maintain focus on overarching goals, even as circumstances evolve. Ultimately, adopting a multi-year framework for metrics supports sustained progress, fosters resilience, and enhances the likelihood of achieving meaningful outcomes aligned with the Equity at Scale (EaS) model.

It is highly advisable for organizations to develop goals and strategies that are easily accessible to the public. Transparent metrics, consistently maintained and regularly updated, are essential for fostering public accountability. When current performance data is readily available, stakeholders—including board members, staff, and the broader community—can better understand organizational progress and challenges.

However, it is important to acknowledge that making goals and metrics public may expose the partner organizations to further scrutiny, particularly if targets are not met due to unforeseeable disruptions. For instance, events such as the COVID-19 pandemic have required significant recalibration of existing objectives. In these circumstances, maintaining open and honest communication with the board and community is imperative. Transparent dialogue helps stakeholders appreciate the external challenges faced by the partner organizations and fosters trust even when outcomes fall short of expectations.

While the aspiration is always to meet or exceed established metrics, falling short should not automatically result in punitive consequences. Instead, unmet goals should be viewed as opportunities for reflection and learning. Lessons drawn from these experiences can inform future strategy, embodying an entrepreneurial mindset that values quick iteration, adaptability, and continuous improvement. This culture of learning and resilience ultimately strengthens the organization's ability to achieve long-term impact and fulfill its mission.

Another important point is to integrate partner organizational objectives into individual and team evaluations is equally important to the success of the EaS model. This approach encourages collective ownership of outcomes, ensuring that every team member, regardless of their specific role or unique metrics, feels engaged and responsible for the organization's overall results. Personal experience has shown that organizational focus intensifies when teams are held accountable for defined goals and metrics.

Lastly, a critical consideration when establishing metrics under the Equity at Scale (EaS) model is finding the right balance between the quantity and quality of performance indicators. There is no universally optimal number of metrics for each type; rather, the focus should be on selecting measures that are both meaningful and actionable.

To achieve this, it is essential to initiate comprehensive discussions with key stakeholders—including board members, partners, philanthropic entities, and the broader community—prior to finalizing any performance indicators. These conversations help ensure that the selected metrics are aligned with the organization's strategic plan, reflect shared priorities, and are relevant to the communities served.

Although this process can be demanding and time-consuming, it is fundamental to organizational success and the effective implementation of the EaS model. Thoughtful engagement with stakeholders not only builds consensus but also fosters a sense of shared ownership and accountability, ultimately strengthening the organization's ability to drive sustainable, equitable outcomes.

For instance, Atlanta's 2020 Economic Mobility Strategy incorporates approximately 35 metrics across four pathways, developed collaboratively with stakeholders to support agency objectives. Accountability for these metrics resides ultimately with the President and CEO of Invest Atlanta, and measurement occurs at both the organizational and individual staff levels. This structure ensures alignment between the agency's mission and its impact, recognizing that collective accountability enhances the likelihood of achieving desired outcomes. Please refer to the Appendix for a comprehensive list of these metrics.

Data Assets

This topic may not be the most captivating, but it holds significant importance due to the potential costs associated with poor monitoring of data assets. Effective data management relies on maintaining consistency and accuracy, ensuring that organizations are able to make reliable comparisons. However, challenges such as managing shared files, file corruption, saving incorrect versions, or remembering to enter data can all impede a successful data management program.

There is no question that the value of data is fundamentally determined by how well it is maintained and its overall accuracy. Inaccurate or poorly managed data can lead to suboptimal decisions, potentially undermining an organization's credibility and resulting in negative financial or reputational consequences. As emphasized by data consultants, ensuring that only accurate and verified information enters the system is crucial for producing reliable results. Conversely, the presence of erroneous or incomplete data will inevitably lead to flawed outcomes and misguided strategies.

Within the Equity at Scale (EaS) model, it is imperative

that teams implement robust data management practices. This includes establishing clear protocols for data entry, regular audits to verify accuracy, and ongoing training for staff responsible for handling data. By prioritizing data integrity at every stage, partner organizations can make informed decisions, demonstrate accountability to stakeholders, and effectively measure progress toward their equity goals.

The dissolution of the California Technology, Trade, and Commerce Agency in 2004 serves as a cautionary example of the critical role that data management and organizational continuity play in sustaining public sector entities. Established in 1992, this agency was California's primary driver for economic development, supporting business growth, employment, infrastructure, and international trade. With a global operational footprint, it actively promoted tourism and foreign investment.

Despite its broad mandate and reach, the agency faced mounting challenges due to budgetary constraints and, more significantly, insufficient and inaccurate data management. When called upon to provide detailed reports on job creation and investment impacts, the agency was unable to supply comprehensive supporting documentation, relying instead on general lists. This lack of detailed records became evident when external parties, such as reporters, cross-referenced agency claims with the companies listed; several companies reported limited or no interaction with the agency regarding relocation assistance.

Compounding these issues, staff turnover resulted in the loss of institutional knowledge and continuity, further exposing the agency to scrutiny and undermining its credibility. The inability to institutionalize the maintenance of accurate and accessible records not only hampered transparency but also left the agency vulnerable during budget reductions and unfavorable media coverage. Ultimately, these factors contributed to the agency's closure and the dismantling of its trade infrastructure.

This case underscores the necessity for rigorous record-keeping and data management protocols. Reliable data is essential for demonstrating impact, responding to stakeholder inquiries, and ensuring organizational resilience. The experience of the California Technology, Trade, and Commerce Agency highlights that inadequate data practices can have far-reaching consequences, including the loss of public trust and the termination of vital programs.

As noted by the Milken Institute the closure of this agency has had a tremendous impact on the state's economy on the generations that followed [38]. If the organization had implemented appropriate data and record-keeping protocols, the closure of the agency might not have been imminent. With proper documentation, the organization could have demonstrated its activities and efforts in response to reports; however, lacking this information, their ability to respond was limited.

Robust data is essential not only for internal decision-making and accountability, but also when seeking funding for program implementation. Funding requests may involve the partner organization's annual budget, programmatic proposals to government entities, private philanthropies, and banking foundations. Regardless of organization type, all partners and funders seek assurance that their investments are achieving meaningful results—a determination that relies on strong data protocols and infrastructure.

Based on this experience, data infrastructure should be regarded as a necessary investment, on par with other critical departments such as finance and compliance. To remain competitive and pursue alternative funding opportunities, organizations must prioritize investments in data systems. A well-developed data infrastructure not only supports accurate reporting and transparency, but also enhances the organization's ability to demonstrate impact, respond to stakeholder inquiries, and adapt to evolving requirements. Ultimately, investing in robust data systems is fundamental to supporting the organization's overall effectiveness and long-term sustainability.

Livable Wage Index

Each data metric can provide valuable insight into the community and its residents. One commonly discussed metric is the livable wage. Since there are multiple approaches to evaluating livable wage, the most compelling are those that have a consideration for wage levels and benefits.

I recommend the Massachusetts Institute of Technology's (MIT) highly regarded Livable Wage Index for work within the United States. While no measurement is without limitations, MIT's methodology is widely considered robust and serves as a valuable reference for policymakers and practitioners. The Livable Wage Index identifies the minimum wage required to achieve a basic standard of living in a given city—essentially, what an individual must earn to support their family through a single job. This consideration is critical to ongoing discussions around the equity work. For example, if a parent must work multiple jobs to provide for their family, data has shown that they often have less time available for their children. In some cases, the lack of time between parent and child can adversely impact the children's academic performance.

Integrating robust data with incentive strategies can significantly influence workforce outcomes and overall organizational results, particularly in the creation of livable wage jobs. For example, when the City of Atlanta intensified its incentives for new business attraction investments and job creation, the city experienced unprecedented corporate growth. Between 2014 and 2021, the number of jobs attracted or retained increased from approximately 5,500 to over 10,000. As the local economy expanded, it became increasingly important to gain a deeper understanding of the labor market, prompting a thorough analysis of the types of positions incentivized.

This review revealed a concentration of high-paying jobs, frequently exceeding $100,000 annually. While these roles are valuable, it became clear that a broader range of employment opportunities was necessary to ensure that all residents could benefit from economic progress. In response, the city broadened its strategic focus to include middle-class job opportunities.

At that juncture, the definition of middle-class earnings in Atlanta was unclear, which led to the adoption of the MIT Livable Wage Index as a benchmark. By comparing wage thresholds with peer cities, the city established an appropriate standard and subsequently launched a program designed to incentivize and attract businesses that create middle-wage positions. The primary objectives of this initiative were to diversify the local economy, increase the availability of middle-wage jobs, and advance equity and economic mobility throughout the city.

Acquiring timely granular city-level data remains a persistent challenge; however, any detailed information gathered at the community level provides enhanced insight into local realities. Tools such as the MIT Livable Wage Index are invaluable in this context, as they enable the development of tailored solutions that address the specific needs of diverse populations. These localized data points help policymakers and practitioners understand what constitutes a livable wage in a given area, ensuring that equitable economic development strategies are both relevant and effective.

Equally important are partnerships with nonprofit organizations, which play a critical role in contextualizing federal or national data for more localized application. Therefore, the nonprofit partners often possess deep knowledge of the communities they serve and can help interpret broad datasets in ways that reflect the lived experiences and unique challenges of local residents. By leveraging these partnerships, organizations can ensure that their programs and incentive structures are responsive to the actual circumstances faced by families and small businesses.

Having access to a variety of data metrics—ranging from national indices to hyper-local surveys—enables organizations to design incentive programs that are truly responsive to the unique circumstances of each community. This approach maximizes the impact of economic development initiatives and supports equitable, sustainable growth by ensuring that all residents have the opportunity to thrive.

Monitoring Results

In order to make informed decisions regarding organizational direction and program development, the significance of robust data cannot be overstated. While most CEOs recognize the critical need for reliable data, it is often surprising that investments—both financial and personnel—in comprehensive data assets, collection, and analysis are not always prioritized or even reflected in organizational budgets. Despite limited resources and significant programmatic demands, allocating funds for data infrastructure is vital. It is highly recommended that such investments should be overseen by a dedicated data manager responsible for daily operations, analysis, information providing, storytelling and overall consistency in reporting across all departments.

Equally essential is the establishment of a centralized system that enables secure and efficient access to organizational data, mitigating the risks of misplacement, accidental deletion or cyber-attack. Instances of inadvertent file modifications or deletions occur frequently; therefore, implementing systems with file protection capabilities and assigning a knowledgeable Information Technology professional to manage these processes is imperative. Without these safeguards, organizations are susceptible to confusion arising from multiple versions of files labeled as "Final," "Final Final," or "Final Final 2."

Accessible and well-managed data not only enhances organizational returns but also facilitates program adjustments based on emerging needs—an integral aspect of the Equity at Scale (EaS) model. Data provides the foundation for determining whether a program, initiative, or organization is effecting positive change. For organizations focused on impact, the presence of clearly defined baselines and metrics is indispensable. The EaS model requires ongoing evaluation, review and adaptation based on measurable outcomes to ensure sustained effectiveness for all those involved.

Checks and Balances

Ronald Reagan's phrase "Trust but Verify" underscores the necessity of compliance offices as internal checks and balances within any organization. In today's environment, transparency is paramount, and organizations are frequently evaluated based on their commitment to openness, transparency and accountability. Effective compliance systems not only appeal to private funders and public partners but also ensure accurate data reporting and uphold program integrity.

My experience managing COVID-19 funding further reinforced the critical importance of involving robust compliance measures from the very beginning of the process. Faced with the pressure to rapidly disburse funds, our team had to design a well-structured application process and maintain accessible documentation that allowed multiple team members to collaborate on files simultaneously. Integrating compliance into the program design at the front end proved essential to the program's overall success.

By anticipating auditor requirements and fostering transparent operations for all stakeholders, we ensured that every aspect of the program was well-documented and easily reviewable. This proactive approach not only streamlined internal workflows but also resulted in the program successfully passing every auditor review. Ultimately, embedding compliance as a core component from the outset safeguarded the integrity of the process, enhanced stakeholder confidence, and supported the delivery of timely and accountable funding

While investing in compliance may sometimes seem thankless and is often targeted during budget reductions, its role is vital—clean audits lead to better reporting and open doors to additional funding opportunities. Strengthening compliance protects an organization's reputation, provides transparency to the public, and enables ongoing success.

For greater protection, hiring external compliance teams can offer unbiased program assessments. During the COVID-19 response, for example, an external group was hired to audit our work as the program was under way. Although this created additional work for our team, it ultimately helped to enhance our reimbursement protocols and document handling processes, effectively preventing any oversight and confusion. The presence of external auditors not only ensured that our procedures met the highest standards but also reinforced stakeholder confidence in the integrity of our operations.

In summary, strong compliance safeguards program delivery and organizational credibility, supporting high-quality services and valuable community impact.

Elevating Customer Service to Advance Equity and Community Engagement

In today's competitive environment, individuals select their place of residence based on a variety of factors. To distinguish themselves from other attractive locations, cities must offer value-added services that enhance resident satisfaction and foster a sense of belonging. Among these, customer service stands out as one of the most effective means for improving resident experience and differentiating a city.

The widespread use of social media platforms has empowered citizens to communicate feedback regarding municipal actions with greater visibility and immediacy. As a result, adopting a customer-focused mindset benefits both residents and municipalities, driving responsiveness and accountability.

Strategies for Enhancing Customer Service and Equity

To improve responsiveness, elevate customer service levels, address equity, and support the Equity at Scale (EaS) model, cities should consider implementing the following strategies:

- Online Chat Functionalities: Enable real-time support and eliminate the need for in-person visits or phone calls, offering flexible access to services.
- Online appointment scheduling with key personnel: Streamline access to city officials and services.

- Expanded access to regional offices: Increase physical accessibility for residents across diverse neighborhoods.
- Off-hour training opportunities: Accommodate residents with nontraditional schedules, such as parents with school-age children or those with demanding work commitments.
- Business advocate office hours: Provide dedicated support for local small businesses navigating municipal processes.
- Appointment of community advocates: Ensure all voices are heard and barriers to services are removed.
- Regular customer surveys about program offerings: Collect timely feedback to inform continuous improvement.
- Adoption of an On-Demand Empowerment model: Empower residents to engage with city resources according to their needs and schedules.

Investing in these initiatives fosters real-time engagement among individuals who may not have previously participated, broadening the reach and impact of community programs.

Equity and the EaS model prioritize meeting people where they are. Tools such as online chat and virtual meetings eliminate barriers to access, enabling individuals to interact with city resources at their convenience. Delivering world-class customer service requires a comprehensive understanding of the population being served. For example, programming limited to traditional business hours may exclude parents, shift workers, or others with unique scheduling needs. Offering virtual and in-person programs after 6 p.m., recording sessions for on-demand access, and providing translation or closed captioning options further enhance accessibility.

Government processes and policies can often be complex and hard to navigate. The addition of roles such as Business Advocate and Constituent Advocate has proven valuable, as these professionals act as primary contacts for stakeholder inquiries and help translate community needs into actionable government responses. A customer service-centric organization also requires infrastructure for immediate feedback collection. Mechanisms such as post-service surveys, QR codes, and regular check-ins ensure that constructive criticism is welcomed and acted upon, driving sustained excellence. The Net Promoter Score serves as an industry benchmark for evaluating customer service. Utilizing recognized metrics allows for transparent performance comparisons within the broader community. For example, at Invest Atlanta, the adoption of this approach has yielded positive results and promoted team accountability.

Robust customer service systems not only facilitate access to available resources but also strengthen organizational responsiveness, accessibility, and accountability. These components are fundamental to the successful implementation of the EaS Model, supporting equitable outcomes and fostering a vibrant, inclusive community.

The Importance of Proactive Communication

One of my college professors once presented the class with a thought-provoking question: "If no one heard or saw the tree fall, did it fall?" This question stimulated a lively 45-minute discussion among students, ultimately illustrating a fundamental principle: the necessity of proactive communication. The exercise made it clear that, in the absence of deliberate and intentional communication, stakeholders and the broader community may remain unaware of your activities. Even more concerning, a lack of clear messaging can lead to the emergence of alternative narratives—some of which may misrepresent your work or intentions.

In today's fast-paced and interconnected environment, it is essential for organizations and individuals to actively communicate their stories, achievements, and objectives. By doing so, they ensure that their efforts are recognized, understood, and accurately represented. Proactive communication not only builds trust and transparency but also safeguards against misunderstandings and misinformation, reinforcing the integrity of the organization's narrative.

During my career, I was tasked with administering a significant grant program for local businesses—one of the largest such programs I have managed. My objective was to ensure that every business in the city was informed about the initiative and its potential benefits. As part of the marketing strategy, funds were allocated for billboard advertising to maximize visibility. I personally visited one of these billboards to document our outreach efforts. However, post-program surveys revealed that fewer than 5% of responding businesses cited billboards as their source of information, whereas social media emerged as the most effective outreach channel. While billboard advertising can be beneficial, for our intended audience, social media yielded superior results.

A diverse communications team—representing various ages, backgrounds, and perspectives—is vital to organizational success, as language, delivery, and cultural understanding significantly influence outcomes. Investing time to tailor messaging for each target group is critical; rarely does a single approach effectively address all interests and needs. Accordingly, customizing communications increases the likelihood of achieving engagement objectives. It is imperative in this field to leverage every opportunity to convey messages in formats accessible and relevant to those who need the information.

For instance, when implementing a home repair program designed to prevent displacement and promote equity, our team identified seniors, single heads of households, veterans, and individuals with disabilities as priority beneficiaries. After finalizing the program guidelines, we strategically selected communication channels based on the preferences and accessibility needs of these groups. Social media served as our primary outreach tool, supplemented by in-person meetings at community centers, presentations at senior facilities, and direct mail campaigns. Recognizing that not all seniors access social media, we intentionally leveraged the networks of family members and caregivers, who often play a critical role in facilitating access to services.

Although it was challenging to pinpoint which outreach method was most impactful, the program's overwhelming response—prompting an early closure due to oversubscription—underscored its success. This outcome was communicated to funders, highlighting the substantial demand and justifying a subsequent phase of the program.

Effective communication is not only necessary for serving communities but also for engaging key stakeholders and decision-makers who influence an organization's capacity to achieve its mission. Below are several communication strategies that have supported both the work of our organization and the implementation of the Equity at Scale (EaS) Model:

Proven Communication Strategies:

- Multi-channel outreach (social media, direct mail, in-person events)
- Tailored messaging for priority groups
- Leveraging caregiver and family networks
- Transparent reporting of program outcomes to funders
- Feedback loops to inform future program phases

By employing a strategic, inclusive approach to communication, organizations can maximize program participation, demonstrate impact, and build trust with both beneficiaries and stakeholders. This commitment to proactive, audience-centered outreach is fundamental to advancing equity and sustaining successful initiatives under the EaS Model.

Building Trust and Consensus Through Community Engagement

After working in Atlanta for approximately two weeks, I

was asked to represent my organization at a neighborhood meeting. Eager to demonstrate my commitment as a team member, I accepted the assignment without hesitation. In retrospect, had I been aware of the challenges ahead, I might have reconsidered.

Following the presentation segment, the meeting transitioned directly into public comment. Several attendees posed general questions or made observations. One resident, Mrs. Taylor, delivered an impassioned critique regarding the organization I had just joined, highlighting actions taken five years prior and directing her inquiries and concerns toward me. Mrs. Taylor expressed her frustration with conviction and intensity. At that time, having only joined the organization a week earlier, I was unfamiliar with either Mrs. Taylor or the specific project referenced. I responded respectfully, stating, "Mrs. Taylor, I hear your concerns and will follow up with you after gathering more information as I am new to this role." Despite my response, she continued to seek answers until those in the audience intervened. Afterward, I approached Mrs. Taylor and invited her for coffee, which she eventually accepted.

During our one-on-one meeting, Mrs. Taylor openly discussed her commitment to her community and her aspirations for its future. This candid conversation left a lasting impression, highlighting that community frustrations often stem from unfulfilled promises rather than personal grievances. It reinforced the importance of relationship-building, active listening, and understanding local perspectives.

Mrs. Taylor has lived in her community since childhood and remains devoted to supporting its development. Empathy toward those we serve fosters mutual investment in equity and progress. Her longstanding advocacy exemplifies this principle. More than ten years later, Mrs. Taylor and I continue to meet regularly for discussions about community needs, shared ideas, and constructive feedback. Our ongoing conversations focus on collaborative problem-solving and positive impact, grounded in honesty and a mutual desire for the community's well-being. Through these exchanges, I have become a trusted advocate and partner.

Individuals like Mrs. Taylor exist in communities nationwide—residents deeply invested in achieving meaningful change. They seek not only to be heard but also to participate actively in shaping outcomes. Securing buy-in for new initiatives depends on integrating community perspectives and feedback. Achieving consensus can be challenging given diverse viewpoints, all deserving consideration. Insights may be gathered through meetings, neighborhood plans, redevelopment strategies, cultural events, media coverage, or stakeholder input.

In Atlanta, Neighborhood Planning Units (NPUs) serve as primary platforms for resident engagement, with city-defined boundaries promoting structured involvement. Additional stakeholders, such as business groups and associations, contribute further perspectives through their participation in the NPU and other local business associations. While aligned opinions expedite decision-making, differing views necessitate careful navigation, often relying on professional judgment and experience.

For younger generations—or those embracing modern tools—social media provides valuable, real-time channels for input. Surveys, QR codes at events, and digital outreach enable ongoing feedback, enhancing communication loops that inform program effectiveness and office engagement.

It is important to pause and reflect on the concept of "community." The term encompasses a diversity of voices, interests, and experiences, and there are often multiple communities within a single geographic area. This heterogeneity enriches our society, and it is essential to create inclusive platforms where everyone is heard and respected. This can be challenging, as those community members who disagree or advocate for alternative strategies are often the most involved, while others who agree may not have the time or ability to attend lengthy meetings. As practitioners, our responsibility lies in seeking common ground and consensus, while ensuring representation of varied perspectives is always taken into consideration. Only by intentionally utilizing multiple engagement methods can we ensure a broad spectrum of voices contributes to community advancement.

The Team

Fostering Trust and Building Effective Teams

No organization is flawless; perfection does not exist. Public and quasi-public entities are frequently held to elevated standards. For instance, the Pew Research Center's Public Trust poll found that only 22% of Americans express trust in the federal government to do the right thing.[39] Given this reality and other factors, it is vital that government and quasi-government representatives subject themselves to rigorous scrutiny, remain open to constructive criticism, and be prepared to analyze feedback and adjust practices when necessary. Transparency must be integral to all aspects of organizational work so that the public can understand agency efforts, objectives, and outcomes.

Much like startups, these organizations must be willing to take measured risks, adapt swiftly, and learn from failure —a principle encapsulated by the adage "fail fast." Continual innovation is crucial; otherwise, entities risk stagnation, diminished relevance, and potential obsolescence. Cultivating meaningful participation in community discourse is fundamental to addressing societal challenges and requires recognizing that success is driven by committed individuals, not the entity alone. Building teams comprised of those devoted to serving others and motivated by community betterment is at the core of effective operations. Such team members possess the ability to navigate complex community, business, and political landscapes with purpose beyond financial gain. True leaders within these teams actively engage communities, foster partnerships, and inspire progress through their personal motivation, passion and vision.

Recognizing personal and organizational imperfection, I

remain steadfast in my commitment to promoting equity and positive change. This work demands ongoing dedication; each day presents opportunities to advance the broader mission, which requires an optimistic outlook and perseverance amidst bureaucratic challenges. When individual and collective resolve align, meaningful transformation becomes attainable.

To ensure this culture permeates every level, it is crucial that the leadership team personally engage with prospective employees—from interns to other executives—to assess alignment with the organization's values and mission. These brief yet purposeful conversations focus on understanding the team and candidates' motivations and character, as exemplified by inquiries about qualities not evident on a resume. Such discussions offer valuable insights into someone's core values and their alignment to the organization.

This profession is demanding, requiring individuals who are deeply committed to the mission and willing to invest considerable time and effort, including attending after hour community meetings and navigating complex political environments. It is critical to assemble teams composed of individuals who share lived experiences with the populations served; as well as empathy derived from firsthand understanding shapes organizational improvement and is indispensable in this field.

Diversity—across geography, age, language, and more—enriches organizational perspectives and enhances program development, as I observed after appointing our first Chief Equity Officer. This leadership addition provided new viewpoints on age, ethnicity, and culture, reshaping both strategy and structure of the organization.

I am continually inspired by colleagues who have overcome significant personal challenges to excel in economic and community development. Many hail from humble beginnings, demonstrating profound dedication to empowering others to transcend generational poverty, pursue equity and achieve lasting improvement.

The Enduring Value of Civil Servants in Advancing Equity

All elected bodies are comprised of representatives who serve fixed terms, with some eligible for re-election. Regardless of tenure, there comes a time when each elected official vacates their position. Likewise, all organizations have leadership teams who, while not bound by term limits, eventually retire or transition out of their roles. This reality underscores the essential function of Civil Servants—professionals whose institutional knowledge and continuity sustain long-term strategic initiatives set by their constituencies. By preserving organizational memory and providing stability through leadership changes, Civil Servants play a critical role in ensuring that progress toward long-term goals, such as advancing equity and community well-being, is not lost during periods of transition.

In other words, Civil Servants provide stability and expertise that transcend political and natural occurring transition cycles. Their deep understanding of organizational history, policies, and community needs enables them to guide and implement complex initiatives, ensuring that progress toward equity and other long-term goals is not lost during these transitions in leadership.

Recognizing and valuing the role these individuals play in advancing efforts toward a more equitable society is fundamental to the long-term success of this work. Their commitment, experience, and ability to maintain momentum are critical assets for any organization striving to create lasting, positive change

The Power of Cross-Sector Partnerships

Just before my scheduled presentation, a fellow CEO approached me and remarked, "I'm surprised to see you here." Sensing my reaction, they clarified that they had not expected my interest in engaging with the museum's national association, given my perceived focus on economic and community development. I responded with a smile and asked if they would attend my session; upon their confirmation, I suggested we reconnect afterwards.

During my presentation, I emphasized that economic and community development extends beyond traditional metrics—it encompasses the creation of quality places where individuals desire to live, work, and recreate. Museum operators are integral to cultivating this sense of place, contributing the unique appeal cities strive to foster. I also presented research highlighting the significant economic impact museums generate within urban environments. Museums not only enhance community life but also can drive equitable economic growth, as they are key to telling and shaping the stories of the past, present, and future.

By serving as cultural anchors, museums, as well as other creative institutions, help define a city's identity and foster civic pride. Their programming and exhibitions attract visitors, stimulate local businesses, and create jobs, while also providing educational opportunities and spaces for dialogue. In this way, museums play a vital role in building inclusive, vibrant communities and supporting sustainable economic development.

After the session, my colleague acknowledged that they had not previously considered an economic and community developer's perspective but now fully understood its relevance. This experience underscored the importance of cross-sector partnerships in advancing our objectives.

Collaborative relationships with educational institutions are often self-evident due to their foundational role in child development; however, schools can also be central to downtown revitalization, and many cities rely on the economic activity generated by student populations. Similarly, partnerships with entertainment venues stimulate demand for hospitality services and support local employment. Financial institutions play a crucial role by assisting entrepreneurs, providing housing finance, and leveraging CRA contributions to benefit organizational initiatives.

Engagements with various service providers—including those in childcare, recreation, healthcare, nutrition, and education—are essential to the models I will discuss. Given the diverse missions and audiences of these organizations, multiple strategic relationships may be necessary with similar service providers.

Finally, philanthropic entities should be engaged at both the national and local levels, with attention paid to their specific goals and priorities. It is important to recognize that partnerships may include forms of support beyond funding, such as technical assistance, which can be equally valuable. When mission alignment exists, combining resources can substantially increase collective impact.

Achieving equity requires meeting communities where they are—a challenge that cannot be met in isolation. By fostering cross-sector partnerships and leveraging the strengths of diverse organizations, we can create vibrant, resilient communities that support economic growth and improve quality of life for all residents.

Strategic Partnerships That Drive Equity

It is essential to emphasize the necessity of forming strategic partnerships to drive equity initiatives. No single entity possesses the capacity to undertake this work independently; partners are vital not only for financial contributions but also for their specialized expertise and credibility. Each organization offers distinct capabilities, and the collective strength achieved through collaboration is indispensable.

Frequently, the primary challenge in advancing equity initiatives lies not in identifying suitable partners, but in securing the necessary administrative funding to support collaborative efforts. It is essential to engage initial partners who can effectively facilitate community involvement, deliver their specialized services, and share valuable insights from their past experiences. By leveraging the collective knowledge and expertise of all partners, organizations can significantly enhance the impact and sustainability of equity-focused programs. Once the partnership network is established, it becomes crucial to build a robust foundation grounded in mutual understanding, trust, clearly defined expectations, and transparent processes for setting and evaluating results. This intentional approach ensures that all stakeholders remain aligned and committed to the shared vision, ultimately driving the success of the equity effort.

Hence, the operational structure of these partnerships must be determined promptly. As the saying goes, "Clear accounts lead to long-term friendships," and the African proverb, "If you want to go fast, go alone. If you want to go far, go together." In practice, establishing clear definitions of responsibilities, sources of capital, funder relations and performance metrics will foster sustainable relationships within the broader community.

When considering specific partners, the Equity at Scale model necessitates partnerships encompassing education, security, workforce development, entrepreneurship, business attraction and retention, transportation, and housing, among other areas. As a people-focused framework, the EaS model seeks inclusive representation across all aspects affecting individuals. While commonalities may exist, unique needs within each community must be identified and integrated into the partnership strategy.

Recognizing that organizations are accountable only for their areas of control, the goal of the EaS model is to drive equitable change through shared objectives, unified metrics, and consensus regarding focus areas. Although I have mentioned it before, I want to emphasize the important of a collaborative vision supported by agreed-upon metrics as it ensures proper alignment among partners. Furthermore, establishing these partnerships at the outset is critical, as introducing new partners mid-program may hinder progress if not incorporated appropriately. Experience demonstrates that early collaboration between government, philanthropy, and nonprofit sectors greatly enhances the potential for large-scale impact.

Additionally, a comprehensive network of organizations capable of providing wrap-around services is essential to support individuals holistically. For instance, unforeseen interruptions such as vehicle breakdowns or childcare cancellations can impede program participation. Incorporating elements like childcare solutions or transportation vouchers can significantly enhance engagement rates. These auxiliary partnerships play a pivotal role in advancing core objectives.

It is also important to address some of the most significant challenges, such as insufficient access to financial services, which adversely affects both businesses and families. This issue is particularly pronounced among Hispanic and African American households in underserved communities. In fact, the Federal Reserve believes that this is not a small issue nationally, but rather one that impacts approximately 4.2 % of the population or 5.6 million households who are unbanked or underbanked.[40] High financial costs strain families who pay more to access capital. The EaS model centers on providing access to services, information, and programs. In some places, banks are plentiful, but in others, like a community I worked in, only payday lenders existed within five miles. Without a bank account, relying on payday loans can result in APRs as high as 400%—unaffordable for anyone.

As for the community in which I was working, there had been several well-intentioned attempts, but none resulted in the establishment of a financial institution. The successful outcome was achieved when the appropriate partnership was formed. In this instance, Tax Increment Financing was utilized to provide financial support for the facility that would eventually host the first community bank. A nonprofit partner played a vital role in funding staffing and administrative expenses. The opening of the first community bank marked a significant milestone, and the institution has now been serving the community from a permanent location for eight years. This collaborative approach demonstrates the importance of collective efforts in addressing significant community challenges such as access to capital. The partners involved were instrumental in effecting positive change for the community and its families in an equitable manner.

The Individual Constituency

One of the foundational attributes of equity is an individual's ability to upskill themselves to earn a higher wage. Organizations such as Goodwill are dedicated to this mission, empowering people through targeted training initiatives. Keith Parker, Executive Director for the Greater Atlanta Area, articulates a clear mission: helping individuals secure employment, advance to better positions, and ultimately build sustainable careers.

Therefore, an effective equity policy should prioritize expanding individuals' skill sets, thereby enhancing their potential to earn higher wages. This approach not only aligns with principles of social responsibility but also yields substantial economic benefits for cities. For example, in an analysis with the Atlanta Regional Commission, we found that in the Atlanta regional economy increasing an individual's earning capacity correlates directly with reductions in income disparity. In fact, a 10% reduction in neighborhood poverty can lead to an average $7,000 rise in family income. In 2018, there were approximately 140,000 families in the Atlanta region living in poverty; reducing this figure by 10% could potentially inject nearly $850 million into the local economy.

Investing in upskilling produces measurable social impacts and simultaneously strengthens the labor pool available to businesses. These outcomes enhance the competitiveness of the Atlanta region, empower current residents, and create pathways for future opportunities. Moreover, such efforts contribute to a more resilient and inclusive workforce, supporting both individual advancement and broader community prosperity.

It is essential to incorporate these calculations and data-driven insights into the broader narrative regarding equity initiatives. As we have mentioned, data serves as an impartial foundation for further discussion, helping stakeholders understand the tangible benefits of investing in skill development—a topic explored in detail within the book's data section.

The Business Constituency

Much of America's development has been shaped by entrepreneurs whose innovative ideas have transformed society —introducing advancements such as the telephone, light bulb, airplane, and blue jeans. Entrepreneurship embodies qualities such as ingenuity, determination, and resourcefulness. Yet, it remains a challenging path, especially for individuals from minority backgrounds who frequently encounter barriers to accessing entrepreneurial resources. Two primary obstacles persist: limited access to financing and targeted technical assistance, both of which are explored in greater detail later in this book.

Research consistently shows that family wealth tends to grow with increased participation in entrepreneurship. Notably, Dr. LaTanya White has introduced the concept of Dynasty Wealth—a framework focused on promoting racial equity within the entrepreneurial ecosystem. She identifies five pillars of Dynastic Wealth, each offering a valuable perspective for this discussion.[41]

1. Financial Wealth: Business and financial assets that form an entrepreneurial dynasty

2. Spiritual Wealth: A greater purpose served beyond mere financial gain

3. Wealth of Knowledge: Rich wisdom and insight gained from life experience

4. Intellectual Wealth: A concerted effort to aid others in developing themselves

5. Relational Wealth: The strength of relationships within one's family and communities

In Dr. White's work, government is recognized as a key player in advancing equity. Federal programming within the education system, housing initiatives, and workforce development programs are highlighted as important levers.[42] Building on this, there is also significant opportunity for local city and

county governments to develop and support similar programming tailored to these communities. An example of this type of
local initiative is provided in the case study section of this book.

Closing the Loop: Communication, Feedback and Equitable Access

Throughout this work, I have emphasized the critical importance of incorporating community feedback into program
development. Equally vital, however, is the need for effective communication—ensuring that program opportunities and
outcomes are clearly conveyed to all stakeholders and that a
continuous feedback loop is maintained. In today's crowded
information landscape, countless organizations and initiatives
vie for the attention of individuals and communities. While
businesses often dedicate significant resources to understanding their audiences—investing in market research, focus groups,
and targeted outreach—government and nonprofit organizations typically operate with far more constrained budgets. As
a result, essential tools such as focus group surveys are rarely
included as line items in governmental budgets, despite their
proven value.

Nevertheless, public sector entities face challenges re-
markably similar to those encountered by their private sector
counterparts when it comes to capturing and retaining audience
attention. The difference lies in the resources available: with
limited funding for marketing and outreach, government and
nonprofit organizations must adopt strategic, creative, and cost-
effective approaches to ensure their messages are heard.

One impactful measure I implemented was the introduction of a customer survey tool at the conclusion of each
program. By asking targeted questions—such as "How did you
hear about us?" and "What can we do better?"—we were able to
track evolving trends in how our audience receives information
and identify areas for improvement. Notably, recent responses
revealed that a significant share of applicants now cite social
media as their primary source of information about our programs. In response to this insight, when launching a small busi-

ness initiative, we strategically reallocated our modest billboard advertising budget to fund a targeted social media campaign. This shift not only maximized our reach and engagement but also demonstrated the value of data-driven decision-making in public sector communication.

Importantly, while digital outreach has become increasingly effective, we have not abandoned traditional methods. We continue to send postcards to every business in the city regarding grant opportunities, recognizing that direct mail remains a reliable and efficient way to reach business owners who may not be active on digital platforms. This blended approach—combining innovative digital strategies with proven traditional outreach—ensures that no group is left behind.

In alignment with the Equity at Scale (EaS) model, our objective is twofold: to guarantee that all business owners have equitable access to essential information, regardless of their preferred communication channel, and to ensure that the feedback we receive directly informs the development and refinement of future programs. By closing the loop between outreach, participation, and continuous improvement, we foster a more inclusive, responsive, and effective ecosystem—one where every voice is valued and every opportunity is accessible.

The Role of the Board of Directors

Every organization is anchored by a board of directors—a group of individuals deeply committed to the organization's mission and supportive of the CEO and implementation team. While communication approaches with the board may differ from one organization to another, my experience has shown that maintaining transparent, consistent, and proactive dialogue is essential for building trust and achieving organizational goals.

Proactive communication is especially important when addressing significant developments or potential challenges. By sharing important updates before they become widely known, leaders can foster a culture of openness and prevent misunderstandings or surprises. This approach not only builds credibility but also ensures that the board remains a reliable partner in navigating complex or sensitive issues.

A key aspect of effective board engagement is taking the time to thoroughly understand each board member or stakeholder. This includes learning their preferred methods of communication—whether by phone, text, email, or other channels—the ideal frequency of contact, and the level of detail they expect. Such awareness is fundamental for driving change, building consensus, and collaborating effectively on complex or controversial initiatives.

In practice, I recommend erring on the side of over-communication, supplemented by timely check-ins. For example, prior to board meetings that will address contentious projects or major decisions, I make it a point to reach out individually to each board member. This ensures they have received all pertinent information, provides an opportunity to respond to any questions or concerns, and allows for further discussion as needed. The objective is to guarantee that no board member is unprepared or uninformed. Exemplary CEOs and executive leaders consistently take these proactive steps to remain aligned with their boards and to foster a sense of shared purpose.

Admittedly, this level of engagement can be challenging —especially for organizations with large or diverse boards, or when the CEO is balancing numerous demands on their time. However, it remains an essential responsibility of organizational leadership. Each stakeholder should feel recognized, valued, and integral to the organization's objectives. When board members are well-informed and engaged, they are better equipped to provide meaningful guidance, support, and oversight.

Ultimately, the board of directors serves as a crucial pillar of support and accountability. By ensuring their informational needs are met and by cultivating strong, transparent relationships, the CEO strengthens both the durability and effectiveness of the organization. This is particularly important when implementing innovative models such as the Equity at Scale (EaS)

Model, where alignment, trust, and clear communication are foundational to long-term success.

The Role of Funders

Funders play a pivotal role in the operation and sustainability of any organization by providing the financial support necessary for programming and growth. Much like the practices adopted by boards of directors, it is essential to keep funders informed—regardless of whether updates are positive or negative. Funders are often individuals or groups who share a deep alignment with the organization's mission and provide ongoing support over time. Maintaining regular, transparent communication helps build trust and ensures that these relationships remain strong.

Funders typically value observable progress, measurable outcomes, and consistent action. Organizations that demonstrate reliability in service delivery, emphasize compliance, and communicate effectively are far more likely to secure continued or additional funding. By sharing clear reports on achievements, challenges, and lessons learned, organizations reinforce their credibility and demonstrate stewardship of the resources entrusted to them.

Beyond their financial contributions, funders also serve as key stakeholders who can validate an organization's effectiveness and impact. Retaining existing funders is often a sign of successful operations and program delivery. In today's competitive funding environment, it is crucial to maintain professional relationships, fulfill commitments, and provide thorough reporting on both outcomes and processes. Meeting these objectives not only supports the retention of current funders but also strengthens efforts to engage new ones.

Ultimately, funders are more than financial supporters—they are partners in the organization's mission. By prioritizing transparency, accountability, and ongoing dialogue, organizations can foster lasting relationships that drive sustained impact and enable continued progress toward their goals.

The Power of National Partnerships

As John F. Kennedy once stated, "Partnership is not a posture, but a process—a continuous process that grows stronger each year as we devote ourselves to common tasks." These words remain as relevant today as ever, underscoring the enduring importance of strong local and national partnerships in advancing organizational missions and driving meaningful change.

I recognize we have discussed Partnership before, but I believe it is important to note that external, national partners bring distinct viewpoints, specialized knowledge, and valuable expertise to the table. National organizations such as Bloomberg or Rockefeller can offer critical input and a broader perspective, especially during times of crisis or rapid change. For example, during the COVID-19 pandemic, national perspectives and remote collaboration became essential as organizations across the country faced unprecedented challenges. The ability to connect with external experts and peers allowed for the rapid exchange of best practices and innovative solutions.

A notable example of effective partnership occurred when Bloomberg assembled a panel of experts—including economic analysts and workforce training specialists—to support Invest Atlanta in developing an economic mobility strategy. This collaboration facilitated frequent coordination among colleagues nationwide, enabling the sharing of programming updates and lessons learned. The partnership inspired the creation of new initiatives, such as a COVID loan program for affected businesses, which was later converted into a grant. When this approach was shared with other cities, many adopted similar programs, demonstrating the value of observing and adapting successful strategies from different municipalities.

While much attention is given to programs that succeed, it is equally important to examine those that do not yield the desired results. The interactions with Bloomberg provided insight into both effective and ineffective practices from other cities. Identifying specific elements that hinder success can be just as informative as analyzing those that drive positive outcomes. This willingness to learn from failure is a hallmark of the startup ecosystem, where nearly two-thirds of ventures never deliver a positive return to investors. If learning from failure is recognized and valued in that environment, similar expectations should be embraced within the government and nonprofit sectors. Given the responsibility of stewarding taxpayer funds, the innovation may take on a slightly different form as program innovation and spending require an even more careful oversight and a commitment to continuous improvement. Needless to say, the practice of learning from mistakes is one that should be embraced.

Professional networks and partnerships serve as invaluable resources for idea sharing, problem solving, and program implementation. During the COVID-19 response, support from Bloomberg was instrumental in shaping Atlanta's first Economic Mobility Strategy, which prioritized equity and collaboration. The team provided ongoing insight into long-term economic impacts, opportunities to connect nationally with peers, and a range of program ideas to assist communities and businesses. External feedback helped highlight the impact of certain initiatives and encouraged the adoption of effective practices.

Ultimately, successful partnerships are built on complementary skills, mutual respect, and a shared commitment to collective goals. By acknowledging limitations and seeking out national and international partners with diverse strengths, organizations can amplify their impact and drive sustainable, equitable change. The experience with Bloomberg exemplifies how leveraging a national network of colleagues and experts can accelerate innovation, foster resilience, and ensure that communities are better equipped to meet both current and future challenges. Their participation had a profound impact on Atlanta's equity work, demonstrating the transformative potential of collaborative efforts that unite expertise, resources, and shared vision.

The Power of Face to Face

Despite substantial investment in social media, marketing materials, and traditional postcards, nothing is more powerful than sitting down and having a coffee and/or a discussion with someone. This underscores the challenge of standing out amid today's competitive environment for public attention. In response, I recommend engaging a team to visit key commercial corridors in the city, directly interacting with business owners or attending events where the target audience is. Although this approach requires significant time and financial resources, the individual results are much more effective. While not feasible for every program, direct outreach can be an effective method to ensure communities are informed about available resources, can leverage opportunities; more importantly it is an instrument to build trust and engagement.

It is critical, however, to remain vigilant when designing community communication strategies as not all actors have the same positive intentions. For this reason, it is imperative to articulate the opportunity, program restrictions and not over promise impact. At one point, we received a call from a donor interested in covering back taxes for every senior in the city—a potentially transformative opportunity for those on fixed incomes as challenges such as unexpected expenses force many seniors into making difficult financial decisions, often pushing property taxes to a lower priority. This initiative offered significant relief.

When the program was announced, the media coverage generated high volumes of inquiries from seniors seeking more information. We considered developing a webpage for address-based eligibility checks, ensuring no personal details would be exposed. However, a team member astutely identified the risk that malicious actors could exploit this system by compiling addresses and targeting homeowners with fraudulent offers for service. This insight prompted us to instead partner with media outlets to communicate directly: eligible individuals would be notified, and no action was required on their part. Ultimately, over 750 seniors received assistance with their back taxes, preventing situations where modest unpaid bills might jeopardize homeownership.

To mitigate such risks, it is essential to involve information technology professionals in all aspects of program design and implementation. At our organization, the Information Technology (IT) department reviews every system purchase and application to ensure robust security measures to protect both personal information and platform access.

Safeguarding data is a collective responsibility. Organizations across sectors face significant risks when adequate protections are not in place. Importantly, cybersecurity threats often arise from human error, such as staff inadvertently responding to deceptive communications. Therefore, comprehensive security training at all organizational levels is vital. Stewardship of public and partner funds requires a proactive approach to information security, beginning with effective IT training programs.

In summary, the core of a strong Equity at Scale (EaS) Model lies in empowering individuals and businesses to access and engage with programs flexibly and conveniently. The model is intentionally designed to maximize access to resources —whether through in-person, online, or on-demand channels —thereby advancing economic mobility for participants, their families, and employees. By removing barriers and centering the needs of those served, the EaS Model fosters greater inclusion, opportunity, and long-term impact.

Summary of the Equity at Scale Model

The Equity at Scale (EaS) model is a comprehensive blueprint designed to address systemic inequities by making services and opportunities accessible, flexible, and responsive to both individual and community's desire for successful outcomes. It recognizes that lasting change requires a deliberate, collaborative, and adaptive approach, engaging stakeholders at every level. The core principals of the EaS model include:

1. Individual/People-Centric Approach

At the heart of the EaS model is the individual. The framework places people at the center of service delivery, ensuring that programs are tailored to meet unique circumstances, aspirations, and challenges. Rather than offering one-size-fits-all solutions, the model provides a menu of services—such as education, business support, housing, and employment—allowing individuals to select the supports most relevant to their needs.

2. On Demand Empowerment (ODE)

EaS emphasizes accessibility through On Demand Empowerment, which ensures services are available when, where, and how people need them. This includes flexible office hours, distributed service locations throughout the community, and robust online platforms that offer 24/7 access to resources. The ODE ecosystem leverages technology and partnerships to remove barriers related to time and location, empowering constituents to engage with services at their convenience.

3. Collaborative Ecosystem

The model moves beyond reliance on a single organization, instead fostering a collaborative network of mission-aligned partners. These partnerships span government agencies, nonprofits, educational institutions, and private sector entities. By sharing responsibility for resource allocation and service delivery, the ecosystem can address a broader range of needs efficiently and effectively. Collaboration also enables the pooling of expertise, funding, and networks, maximizing impact.

4. Equitable Access

EaS is built on the principle that all community members should have equal access to service providers and opportunities. The model is intentionally designed to minimize barriers—whether related to language, transportation, technology, or awareness—reinforcing fairness and inclusion. Services are differentiated and diversified to address the wide spectrum of needs, wants, and aspirations within the community.

5. Data-Driven and Adaptive

A key feature of the EaS model is its reliance on clear metrics, ongoing monitoring, and stakeholder feedback. Data is used to set benchmarks, measure progress, and inform real-time adjustments to strategies and programs. The model encourages transparency in reporting, continuous evaluation, protection of important information, and the integration of community feedback to ensure that initiatives remain relevant and effective.

6. Sustainability and Scalability

EaS is designed to be both sustainable and adaptable. By balancing limited resources with the pursuit of equity, the model supports long-term, systemic change. Its flexible structure allows for customization based on local context, politics, budget, and community feedback, making it applicable to a wide range of communities and regions.

Some of the implementation highlights of the EaS model are:

- Flexible Service Delivery: Services are offered through multiple channels—physical locations, online portals, social media, and traditional outreach—to ensure broad accessibility.
- Continuous Improvement: Feedback loops and data analysis drive ongoing refinement of programs, ensuring responsiveness to changing needs and circumstances.
- Strategic Partnerships: Early and intentional collaboration with diverse partners is essential for building capacity, sharing expertise, and sustaining impact.
- Clear Metrics: Success is measured using well-defined, transparent metrics that are regularly updated and publicly shared, fostering accountability and trust.

The EaS model provides a scalable, resilient blueprint for communities seeking to close equity gaps and foster lasting, inclusive progress. By centering individuals, leveraging partnerships, and embracing data-driven adaptation, EaS empowers communities to address historic inequities and build pathways to opportunity for all.

The following case studies will further illustrate the real-world impact and practical application of the EaS Model within diverse communities. Each example demonstrates how flexible, people-centered strategies can drive meaningful change and support sustainable progress toward equity.

Key Takeaways for Part 2

To effectively advance equity in your community, focus on meeting individuals where they are by designing programs and outreach strategies that address specific needs and circumstances. This means moving beyond one-size-fits-all solutions and instead tailoring support—whether through flexible service delivery, culturally relevant communication, or targeted technical assistance—to ensure genuine access and participation. Regularly evaluate and adapt your programs based on feedback and changing community dynamics, embrace innovation and collaboration across sectors, and use data-driven insights to guide decisions and measure impact. Most importantly, empower communities by engaging stakeholders authentically, making their voices central to every initiative, and fostering a culture of continuous improvement. By integrating these principles, you can create responsive, inclusive, and sustainable solutions that close opportunity gaps and help all community members thrive.

PART III:

THE EQUITY BLUEPRINT, CASE STUDIES

Throughout this book, I have explored how a wide range of publications and analyses have demonstrated the profound impact that policies—both past and present—have had on communities, often limiting opportunities for economic mobility and perpetuating inequities. Despite these challenges, there is a growing community of dedicated professionals in the economic and community development field who are committed to driving positive change and supporting the advancement of these communities and their future generations.

Yet, a fundamental question persists: how and where should equity work begin? While it would be ideal to offer a definitive, step-by-step roadmap to success, the reality is that no universal solution exists. Each community is shaped by its own distinct identity, history, and culture, which means that advancing equity requires approaches tailored to local context. There is no single method that fits all situations. Hence my attempt to leave you with a blueprint that you can use to shape the equity in your community.

Nevertheless, there are best practices and proven strategies that can inform the development of effective equity initiatives. Drawing from extensive experience across diverse markets, I present a series of examples and practical approaches throughout this book to encourage communities to address existing inequities with intention and creativity. Although the work is complex and often challenging, identifying areas for broad collaboration is essential. The Equity at Scale (EaS) model is designed to deliver mutually beneficial outcomes, and these collaborative actions are vital not only for establishing credibility but also for building sustained community support for equity-driven efforts.

Launching equity work often begins with focusing on opportunities that are readily attainable—those "low-hanging fruit" that can be addressed quickly and effectively. By communicating progress, even if incremental, and leveraging early successes, communities can build momentum and lay the groundwork for larger, more ambitious initiatives. Addressing immediate opportunities creates a strong foundation for tackling more complex challenges in the future, which, while demanding greater effort, yield substantial rewards and lasting impact.

Accessible opportunities also serve as catalysts for aligning with strategic partners. Collaboration with individuals and organizations—whether through action, advocacy, or funding—can amplify the reach and effectiveness of equity initiatives. Therefore, it is crucial to cultivate a robust network of stakeholders who are committed to contributing their expertise, resources, and energy to the cause. By fostering these partnerships and maintaining open channels of communication, communities can create an environment where equity work is not only possible, but sustainable and transformative.

Ultimately, the journey toward equity is ongoing and requires adaptability, perseverance, and a willingness to learn from both successes and setbacks. By embracing best practices, leveraging early wins, and building strong collaborative networks, communities can make meaningful progress toward closing equity gaps and creating opportunities for all.

A Tale of Two Atlantas: Prosperity, Disparity and the Path Forward

When considering early economic growth factors for Atlanta, two crucial events come to mind. In 1837, the Western and Atlantic Railroad companies established Atlanta as a rail distribution center, and in 1881, the International Cotton Exposition arrived in the city. The results of these decisions and investment put Atlanta at the center of manufacturing and commerce by the end of the nineteenth century.[43] Clearly, transportation was a key industry cluster for the city; and the establishment of Hartsfield-Jackson International Airport in 1925 further solidified this position on a national scale.

Atlanta currently ranks fourth in the nation for its concentration of Fortune 500 companies. The city's distinguished roster is notable for its diverse business sectors, setting Atlanta apart from other metropolitan areas. Additionally, the presence of Historically Black Colleges and Universities within Atlanta significantly contributes to workforce diversity and serves as a vital component of the local economy.

Despite Atlanta's many strengths, one key statistic underscores the importance of implementing an equity strategy: the latest U.S. Census Bureau report on income inequality. This analysis utilized the Gini coefficient as its primary metric. The Organization for Economic Co-operation and Development (OECD) defines the Gini coefficient as "the comparison of cumulative proportions of the population against the cumulative proportions of income they receive[44] In other words, the Gini coefficient will measure the income distribution in a\population. The coefficient ranges from 0 (perfect equality) to 1 (perfect inequality).

In the U.S. Census Bureau's data from the 2016-2020

American Community Survey data, the City of Atlanta ranked the worst among other peer cities with more than 100,000 inhabitants. This means income disparity between the rich and poor in Atlanta is greater than other cities with similar size.[45]

The following visualization illustrates the racial and economic distribution of Atlanta neighborhoods. By examining the relationship between race and income across these areas, distinct patterns can be observed. Each dot in the scatterplot represents a Neighborhood Statistical Area (NSA). The majority of neighborhoods are positioned at the bottom right or top left of the graph, with few appearing elsewhere, indicating that many neighborhoods tend to have a relatively uniform racial composition. The color of each dot reflects the median household income for the corresponding neighborhood. This shows how NSAs with a majority non-Hispanic Black population tend to have considerably lower median household incomes (in red) than NSAs with a predominantly non-Hispanic white population (in blue). [46]

Race and Income

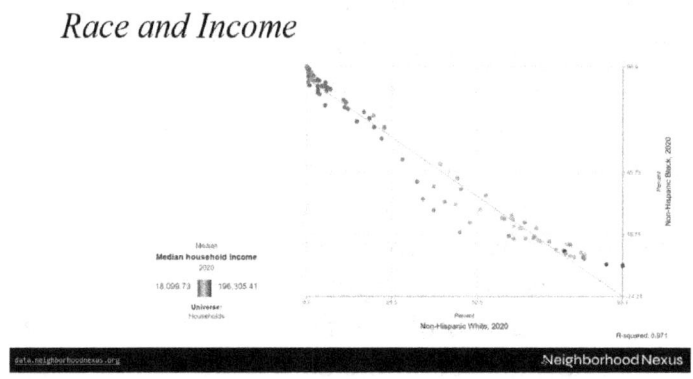

Figure: 3.1 Racial and economic distribution

Based on Neighborhood Nexus' research, there is no doubt that the City needs a strategy focused on equity-based policies and programs that can begin to address the many years of disinvestment within the City.

Removing Barriers and Building Opportunity:

A Commitment to Inclusive Growth

Invest Atlanta serves as the City's economic development agency, providing a comprehensive portfolio of programs focusing on economic growth, community development, and engagement. The scope of Invest Atlanta's initiatives within these departments is extensive, including the management of eight active tax increment financing districts, known in Georgia as Tax Allocation Districts (TADs). Oversight of these districts involves program creation, application review, fund disbursement, and compliance monitoring—a process managed by Invest Atlanta since its inception.

With the establishment of the first economic development strategy centered on economic mobility, Invest Atlanta expanded and refocused its programming per Invest Atlanta's Economic Mobility Strategy: Pathways to Success:

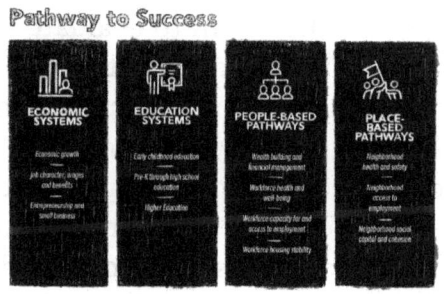

Figure 3.2 Pathways to Success

Advancing this new Neighborhood strategy necessitated a deliberate reassessment of existing approaches and a commitment to continuous improvement. The team recognized that meaningful progress in economic mobility for these neighborhoods required ongoing evaluation, identification of opportunities, and careful consideration of potential unintended consequences.

A relevant analogy illustrates this shift in perspective: just as a child may believe they have adequately cleaned their room by addressing only surface-level tasks, organizations must also assess whether their well-intended actions truly achieve optimal outcomes. This recognition prompted Invest Atlanta to expand the staffing capacity and engage a third-party consultant to conduct rigorous program reviews.

As part of this commitment to excellence, Invest Atlanta commissioned an independent analysis of its program fund distribution. Contractors reviewed awardees across various projects, paying particular attention to ethnic diversity. Notably, although many funded projects were located in historically Black neighborhoods—such as Sweet Auburn and Edgewood—the proportion awarded to minority-owned businesses was unexpectedly low. Further examination revealed that while grants had been provided to minority project owners, there had been no denials of minority applications, highlighting a lack of minority applicants rather than bias in the approval process.

This discovery led the team to evaluate the accessibility and effectiveness of the program. Despite a rolling call for projects, minority organizations were not submitting applications, raising questions about underlying barriers. To address this, Invest Atlanta collaborated with Central Atlanta Progress, the local community improvement district, conducting outreach through surveys, corridor walks, and community meetings to gather input and understand the impact of program requirements.

Field observations indicated that property ownership within TADs often resided with religious entities, which, although asset-rich, frequently lacked development expertise and sufficient cash flow. Typically, these institutions do not hold sizeable endowments or possess staff specialized in large-scale development. Application requirements—including architectural renderings, Environment Impact Reports (EIR) Phase 1, and capital stack analyses—represented significant financial investment, potentially exceeding $50,000, which posed a challenge for many applicants.

In response, Invest Atlanta re-evaluated its application

criteria to distinguish essential documentation from optional requests, recognizing its responsibility to manage taxpayer funds judiciously and maximize community impact. Feedback highlighted that stringent requirements disproportionately affected the intended beneficiaries. Consequently, the team introduced a Pre-Development Loan Fund, offering smaller loans to mitigate risk and facilitate access to larger funding opportunities. The loan structure ensured minimal financial burden, integrating seamlessly into project financing.

Although not without risk, this initiative successfully increased participation among minority developers. Furthermore, collaboration with partners resulted in a support network of architects and financial consultants to assist religious organizations, empowering more community members to engage in local development.

This example underscores the necessity of thorough and intentional program analysis to identify potential issues and challenges. Had Invest Atlanta ceased its efforts at initial findings, core problems would have persisted. Organizations are encouraged to remain receptive to identifying obstacles to program success and to collaborate with external stakeholders capable of uncovering unintended consequences.

Nourishing Equity: Innovative Strategies
for Fresh Food Access

Food desserts are a national problem. The U.S. Drug Administration estimates that 6.1% – 18.8 million people – live more than one mile from a supermarket.[47] And obesity rates now affect "about 1 in 5" children in the United States.[48] There are numerous studies that build a completing case for the benefits of access to fresh foods, such as lower obesity rates and better performance in schools. The research overwhelmingly demonstrates a direct correlation between diet and academic achievement.[49]

Food deserts exist despite the importance of fresh food access for economic mobility, community wellbeing and the overall social determinants of health. The reasons for their presence in urban markets vary by region, but they commonly include:

- Crime or the perception of crime
- Limited availability of large development sites
- Low disposable income among residents
- Higher development and operating costs
- Traditional market data not capturing full economic potential
- Limited access to financing
- Educational attainment

Grocery retailers typically avoid risk and are unlikely to be early entrants in unestablished urban markets. Attracting these retailers to underserved communities often requires significant economic measures including tax abatements, grants, and various incentives. While businesses operate based on their respective models, aligning a retailer's approach with city needs, or implementing alternative solutions, can address immediate demand for groceries. Most community members prioritize access to quality fresh produce over the specific brand of retailer.

Efforts to reduce food deserts in Atlanta have led to progress, but many areas still lack access to fresh foods. In 2020, about 25% of Atlantans lived in a food desert, defined as residing more than half a mile from a supermarket. Interstate 20 remains a dividing line for economic mobility within the city, though some northern communities also experience limited access to fresh food, as depicted witin the light grey areas of the map. The darker areas of the map show the radius to the store considering drive and walk times.

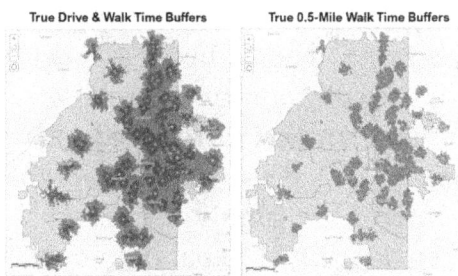

Figure 3.3 Food deserts in the city

With economic mobility as a central focus, a dedicated team developed a comprehensive strategy to address the limited access to fresh food in certain areas of the city. This approach encompasses four primary components:

- Attract major supermarkets and grocery stores to increase access to fresh food, create employment opportunities, and encourage new investment within the community.
- Retain community-oriented local stores, as they continue to provide essential food access and serve as important sources of employment.
- Expand and enhance corner and neighborhood markets that demonstrate commitment to the community and possess strong market potential but face identifiable challenges.
- Explore innovative food access models designed to address immediate community needs.

For each strategic component, the team established roadmaps to overcome barriers to entry, ranging from targeted outreach to national grocers and conducting site visits, to creating neighborhood profiles and identifying available development sites. In collaboration with the City Council and Mayor's office, the team introduced several new incentives and expanded existing programs, such as the Commercial Improvement Grant Incentive—offering funding for store improvements—and the Middle Wage Job Fund, which supports local hiring initiatives that benefit both the community and retailers. Additionally, an Expanded Loan Program was introduced to support supply acquisition and expansion efforts under favorable terms. Collectively, these incentives are highly attractive to both large and small retailers considering or expanding operations within the city.

A willingness to think ambitiously, embrace innovation, and take measured risks has been fundamental to advancing solutions for food deserts in Atlanta. The city's commitment to addressing this critical issue is evident in the launch of two municipal grocery stores—one located in downtown Atlanta, which opened in Q3 2025, and another in Southwest Atlanta, scheduled to open in Q1 2026. These stores represent more than just new retail locations; they are the result of sustained collaboration between city leadership, including the Mayor and City Council, and a broad coalition of community stakeholders. The process required navigating complex logistical, financial, and regulatory challenges, but the anticipated impact on local families is profound. By providing reliable access to fresh, healthy foods, these stores are poised to improve nutrition, support local economies, and foster greater equity for residents who have long faced barriers to food security.

Beyond these flagship projects, the city has pursued a range of short-term strategies to accelerate progress. Strategic partnerships have been instrumental, bringing together organizations such as MARTA, Georgia Tech, Atlanta Food Bank, Goodr, and Urban Farmers. These collaborations have enabled the development of creative, community-driven solutions—ranging from mobile food markets and pop-up produce stands to educational initiatives and urban agriculture programs. By leveraging the expertise and resources of diverse partners, including the Independent Grocers Alliance, the city has been able to pilot innovative approaches, adapt quickly to emerging needs, and build trust within the community.

Initially, efforts focused on engaging large grocery developers to anchor these initiatives. However, as the program evolved, it became clear that partnering with local grocers whose missions aligned with the city's equity goals offered greater potential for sustainable impact. These relationships have not only expanded access to healthy foods but also strengthened the local business ecosystem, creating new opportunities for entrepreneurship and community investment.

In summary, Atlanta's approach to eliminating food deserts demonstrates the power of bold vision, collaborative action, and adaptive strategy. The opening of municipal stores, coupled with innovative partnerships and a focus on local alignment, is transforming the landscape for families across the city—ensuring that equitable access to nutritious food becomes a reality for all.

Strategic Program Design and Implementation

In 2015, the Invest Atlanta team came together to explore ways in which they, as the city's economic and community authority, could implement a strategy that would support the legacy residents in the city. The goal was to provide a pathway for these legacy residents to stay in their homes and not be displaced. Several reports, including one from the Atlanta Regional Commission, highlighted the rise in the Atlanta Metropolitan region's growth rate. In fact, the region's job employment base increased 8% since 2020 representing the seventh-highest rate in the nation among major metro areas.[50] We knew that something had to be done. With the employment rate up so to would the demand on housing.

Following extensive consultation with both internal teams and community stakeholders, we identified multiple avenues through which our organization could meaningfully address housing stability for vulnerable populations. After careful evaluation, two primary interventions were prioritized: owner-occupied rehabilitation and targeted tax assistance. Both programs are currently operational and have demonstrated measurable impact. For the purposes of this case study, I will focus on the owner-occupied rehabilitation initiative, which closely aligns with the On Demand implementation strategy discussed earlier in this manuscript.

The Owner-Occupied Rehabilitation program was conceived to address critical health and safety repairs for homeowners, particularly seniors living on fixed incomes who often lack the resources to maintain their residences. Recognizing the intersection of housing stability and community well-being, the program provides eligible homeowners with up to $30,000 in funding for essential repairs to major home systems. Financial assistance is structured as a deferred, forgivable loan with a 0% interest rate, repayable only under specific circumstances such as sale, transfer of ownership, or failure to maintain primary residency during the term of the loan. The principal balance is reduced annually by 10% or 20%, contingent upon continued occupancy, thereby incentivizing long-term stability and minimizing financial burden.

During the program's inaugural year, our approach emphasized individualized engagement. Staff conducted in-depth consultations with senior homeowners to identify a broad spectrum of repair needs, ranging from fencing and driveways to roofing, plumbing, and kitchen renovations. While this comprehensive scope was well-intentioned, it quickly became apparent that managing such a wide array of services posed significant operational challenges. The diversity of repair requests required a large pool of contractors with varied expertise, complicating project management and budget allocation.

A specific example illustrates this complexity: one homeowner requested an iron fence replacement, which, while addressing a legitimate safety concern, would have consumed a disproportionate share of available resources. Through collaborative dialogue, we were able to negotiate with the homeowner to address major roofing and HVAC issues that posed greater risks to habitability.

In response to these operational challenges, the program underwent a strategic redesign. The revised model standardized the menu of eligible services, focusing on repairs with the greatest impact on health, safety, and housing longevity—namely, roof replacement, major system repairs. Homeowners retained the option to petition for additional repairs outside this scope, though such requests were subject to stringent review and limited approval.

This targeted approach yielded several key benefits:

1. *Enhanced Clarity for Homeowners*: By narrowing the range of services, homeowners could more easily understand their options and make informed decisions about which repairs would best serve their needs.

2. *Cost Efficiency and Resource Optimization*: Standardization enabled the organization to leverage bulk pricing and negotiate favorable terms with contractors, thereby increasing the number of residents served within existing budget constraints.

3. *Workforce Development*: With a defined set of repair categories, we look to partner with training providers to upskill local workers, ensuring a ready pool of qualified workers and supporting broader economic development goals.

4. *Accelerated Service Delivery*: Streamlining the program reduced administrative complexity and shortened project timelines, allowing us to decrease the average wait time for repairs by half the time.

The evolution of the owner-occupied rehabilitation program underscores the importance of continuous improvement and adaptive management in public service delivery. By focusing on high-impact services and operational efficiency, we were able to expand program reach, improve cost-effectiveness, and enhance outcomes for vulnerable homeowners. The experience also reinforced a critical lesson: responsiveness to community needs and agility in program design are essential for sustaining housing stability and enabling residents to remain in their homes.

Ultimately, this case study demonstrates that targeted interventions, informed by stakeholder feedback and data-driven analysis, can significantly advance equity and resilience within communities. As demand for such programs continues to grow, ongoing evaluation and strategic refinement will be vital to maximizing impact and ensuring long-term sustainability.

Strategic Scoring: Leveraging the Neighborhood Equity Index for Inclusive Growth

In March 2020, Invest Atlanta identified significant challenges faced by the city's small businesses due to the COVID-19 lockdown. The business landscape shifted abruptly, and there was uncertainty regarding the duration of these conditions. Recognizing the difficulties experienced by local businesses, the team proposed a small business loan fund to the City Council and Mayor. A $1 million allocation was approved to establish the Business Continuity Loan Fund (BCLF), offering no-interest loans with flexible repayment terms. This initiative aimed to enable small businesses to endure the disruption. Through dedicated efforts, the funding was distributed within weeks, although it soon became apparent that ongoing pandemic restrictions would further complicate recovery.

As the pandemic unfolded, Invest Atlanta received additional allocations from the City of Atlanta's CAREs Act and American Rescue Plan Act funds, specifically aimed at supporting small businesses. While rapid deployment of resources was essential, it soon became clear that these funds were not adequately reaching the city's disinvested neighborhoods—areas historically underserved and facing persistent barriers to economic opportunity.

To address this gap, Invest Atlanta leveraged its comprehensive economic development strategy, the One Atlanta: Economic Mobility, Recovery and Resiliency Plan. This plan is designed to expand economic opportunities for all residents, with a particular focus on equity and inclusion based on 4 Pathways to Success: Economic Systems, Education Systems, People Based and Place Based, see below:

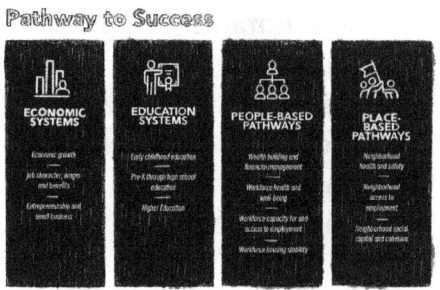

Figure 3.4 Pathways to Success

A cornerstone of this strategy was the creation of a Neighborhood Equity Index, which incorporated 26 people- and place-based indicators—such as third grade reading proficiency and transportation access—to assess the overall score of each Neighborhood Statistical Area. Areas with lower scores were designated as "disinvested," and this mapping tool enabled the city to prioritize investments, shifting focus from high-investment (green) to low-investment (red) zones.

Building on this foundation, the program team collaborated with legal advisors to revise scoring metrics and implement equity-based evaluation criteria. The updated matrix placed greater emphasis on small businesses located in disinvested neighborhoods, integrating the Economic Mobility Index directly into the grant decision-making process. Each applicant's address was cross-referenced with the index map, and additional variables—such as race, gender, and other equity considerations—were factored in. As a result, applicants from underserved communities received higher weighted scores, as detailed in Appendix GC-1.

These changes led to a significant increase in support for small businesses in disinvested areas. While the CAREs Act segment of the program allowed nearly all eligible applicants to receive awards, the true challenge emerged during the American Rescue Plan phase, where funding was more limited and competition intensified.

The outcomes were notable: the proportion of approved applicants from disinvested neighborhoods rose from 16% under the BCLF, to 17% during the first round of the Resurgence program and then surged to 52% in the second round of Resurgence. The accompanying map visually illustrates these results, with blue dots representing funded businesses and red, orange, and yellow regions highlighting the targeted neighborhoods.

This data-driven, equity-focused approach not only increased access to critical resources for small businesses in Atlanta's most vulnerable communities but also sets a precedent for how targeted strategies and transparent metrics can drive meaningful change.

Figure 3.5 Impact of equity focused scoring

The key takeaway is that effective economic mobility initiatives should integrate data throughout the decision-making process. In this instance, the Economic Mobility Index informed and achieved our objective: increasing the number of small businesses in disinvested neighborhoods that received essential, limited grant funding. By intentionally applying equity data, we delivered meaningful benefits to these communities. Ultimately, through data-driven and equity-based scoring, Invest Atlanta nearly tripled the number of funded small businesses in underserved areas, advancing the city's equity goals and ensuring grants were allocated where they were most needed. These outcomes depended on the Equity Index.

Embedding Equity in Business Attraction:
The E3 Matrix Approach

As previously noted, economic developers often strive for top rankings across industry lists—except, notably, in the area of income inequality, where Atlanta consistently remains among the top two cities nationwide. Recognizing the urgency of this challenge, the city has made a firm commitment to address income inequality head-on. In alignment with this commitment, Invest Atlanta applies an equity lens to all its initiatives, ensuring that every program and policy is evaluated for its potential to advance equitable outcomes.

To further this goal, Invest Atlanta undertook a comprehensive review of its core programs, including the critical area of business attraction. Atlanta competes on both national and international stages for limited investment and employment opportunities, with factors such as time zone, geographic location, workforce, transportation accessibility and tax environment all influencing outcomes. The challenge was clear: design a program that would keep Atlanta competitive without compromising the city's core values or its mission to foster a more equitable community. The team was determined to find a solution that balanced competitiveness with a steadfast commitment to equity.

After extensive consultation with companies, community representatives, and regional economic developers, the team developed the Economic Empowerment and Equity (E3) matrix. This framework, illustrated in graphs GC-2, outlines clear expectations for any new company seeking to establish operations in Atlanta. The E3 matrix serves as an entry point into the "Atlanta Way," encouraging companies to contribute positively to the city's social and economic fabric. The approach is straightforward: while Atlanta welcomes all companies, those seeking city-sponsored incentives must commit to advancing equity goals through a tailored E3 plan.

The E3 matrix offers a menu of potential commitments, allowing companies to select actions that align with their unique objectives and capacities. This flexibility ensures that organizations of varying sizes and sectors can participate meaningfully. To facilitate adoption, Invest Atlanta provides guidance to companies as they navigate the matrix, often uncovering synergies with existing corporate social responsibility or ESG (Environmental, Social, and Governance) initiatives. In today's business environment, many companies are already familiar with such requirements, making the transition smoother and more impactful.

At its core, the E3 matrix is designed not only to create jobs but to ensure those positions offer fair wages, robust benefits, and opportunities for advancement. The framework supports employment across a range of pay scales, encourages upskilling as a pathway to economic empowerment, and advocates for partnerships with nonprofit, educational, and philanthropic organizations. This collaborative, multi-sector approach is essential for driving sustainable progress and maximizing community benefit.

After a year of implementation, the E3 matrix continues to evolve in response to stakeholder feedback and changing economic conditions. While one organization opted out due to perceived complexity, the majority have embraced the initiative and made meaningful commitments. Evaluating the full impact on business attraction will require several years of data and analysis. However, the early results are promising, and broader adoption of similar value-driven frameworks by other cities could enhance competitiveness while advancing shared civic goals and principles.

In summary, the E3 matrix represents a bold step forward

in embedding equity into Atlanta's economic development strategy. By setting clear expectations, fostering flexibility, and prioritizing collaboration, Invest Atlanta is helping to ensure that growth and opportunity are accessible to all residents—laying the groundwork for a more inclusive and prosperous future.

Communicating for Change: Equity Focused Outreach

With an area exceeding 20,000 square miles, San Bernardino County stands as the largest county in the United States by land. This vast expanse presents both significant opportunities and unique challenges for economic development initiatives. My experience in this region underscored the pivotal role that a robust marketing and communications program plays in informing, engaging, and mobilizing community members. While residents were generally familiar with the county's core responsibilities, there was a notable gap in awareness regarding its economic development activities.

To address this, I collaborated with then-CEO Brian McGowan to develop a new logo for the organization, focusing on creating a brand identity that reflected the county's distinctiveness. Our outreach efforts extended beyond local boundaries, encompassing increased engagement both within and outside the county. We launched an intensive advertising campaign and sponsored several national events, all of which elevated our visibility and strengthened our ability to connect with target audiences. Some of the key lessons and best practices included:

- Comprehensive Engagement: Effective equity strategies require a strong marketing and communications component. Given the involvement of numerous partners, stakeholders, and participants, it is essential to ensure comprehensive engagement and transparent information sharing at every stage.
- Partner Awareness: One critical takeaway is the importance of keeping key partners fully informed. Lapses in communication can undermine both their credibility and the broader strategy, potentially jeop-

ardizing collaborative efforts and long-term impact.

- Leadership Integration: It is advisable to include the head of marketing and communications within senior leadership. This ensures that communications professionals remain current on organizational initiatives and are prepared to manage inquiries from the press or public at any time.
- Brand Identity: Developing a distinct and recognizable brand identity helps unify messaging and fosters a sense of pride and ownership among stakeholders.
- Multi-Channel Outreach: Leveraging a mix of advertising, event sponsorship, and digital engagement expands reach and builds trust with diverse audiences.

In summary, the experience in San Bernardino County demonstrates that strategic marketing and communications are not ancillary functions—they are central to the success of economic development and equity initiatives. By prioritizing transparency, proactive engagement, and leadership integration, organizations can build stronger partnerships, enhance public awareness, and drive meaningful change.

Breaking Barriers: Equity, Opportunity and Community in Los Angeles

I am deeply grateful for Los Angeles—the city where my immigrant parents met and where I spent my formative years. As the youngest and only girl among five siblings, I grew up watching my brothers play baseball, longing to join them on the field. Initially, I was only allowed to be a cheerleader, a role that felt limiting compared to the excitement of the game. That year, I met Jennifer, another talented girl who, like me, was relegated to cheering from the sidelines. At that time, Little League did not allow girls to play. Our shared experience sparked a close friendship and a determination to challenge the status quo.

The following season, thanks to the advocacy of our mothers, the league made the bold decision to go co-ed. Jennifer and I eagerly joined, borrowing gear from our brothers and stepping onto the field with a mix of excitement and nerves. Although our coach was hesitant at first, our performance—especially Jennifer's memorable home run and my rocket arm—quickly proved our abilities. We soon became integral members among a team dominated by boys. Only later did I learn that this change was made possible because Mr. Martinez, one of the coaches, agreed to add girls to his roster. I thank Mr. Martinez for believing in us and gave us a chance to prove what we could do on the field.

These early experiences profoundly shaped my belief in providing opportunities rather than handouts. They taught me that real equity is achieved through creative thinking, advocacy, and a willingness to challenge established norms. In my career with the City of Los Angeles, I experienced, firsthand, that fostering economic mobility requires identifying gaps and developing innovative solutions to bridge them.

As a foundational step in any successful initiative, it is essential to begin by genuinely speaking and listening to the community. This process involves organizing community exercises or brainstorming sessions that foster unrestricted ideation, where every participant feels empowered to share their thoughts and experiences. At the outset, all ideas should be welcomed and considered valid, creating an environment where creativity can truly flourish.

Once ideas have been gathered, the next phase is thoughtful categorization. It is natural for some concepts to overlap or even fall out of scope; documenting these accordingly ensures that no valuable insight is lost and that the process remains transparent. After compiling the full list of suggestions, the focus should shift to prioritizing the most feasible ideas—often referred to as "low hanging fruit." By targeting these actionable opportunities first, organizations can generate goodwill, demonstrate early success, and build momentum within the community.

This approach has consistently proven effective in establishing trust, encouraging ongoing participation, and laying the groundwork for more ambitious, long-term goals. By valuing every voice and acting on achievable ideas, leaders can foster a sense of shared ownership and collective progress.

During my time working with Council Member Alex Padilla, I was frequently invited to accompany him on district drives to gain firsthand insights into local conditions. These drives often included impromptu stops to engage directly with residents, many of whom knew Alex personally. He consistently took the time to inquire about their wellbeing and any immediate needs, reinforcing the importance of genuine community engagement.

My experiences with the Council Member underscored a vital lesson: community members and business owners are often best positioned to identify their neighborhood's most pressing needs—provided someone takes the initiative to ask. On one occasion, I can remember the Council Member driving me directly to an undeveloped site in Sylmar. I asked him why we were looking at an undeveloped piece of property. He paused and asked for my opinion on the potential of establishing a children's museum at that location. Initially, I was skeptical, given at the time Sylmar had a dearth of retail amenities and foot traffic—characteristics typically sought by museums. However, I soon recognized the Council Member's propensity for innovative thinking. While his suggestion seemed unconventional, it reflected his commitment to exploring new possibilities for community improvement.

These collective experiences have reinforced my conviction that meaningful change is possible when we listen, innovate, and remain open to new ideas—no matter how unconventional they may seem at first.

It's likely that the Council Member reviewed information about how early education affects a child's economic mobility. According to a Harvard study, children enrolled in early childhood education programs were less likely to be held back in school and more likely to graduate from high school.[51] In other words, the positive impact of early childhood education programs is crucial to the ability for a low-income child to break out of the cycle of poverty. In fact, studies have shown that the long-term impact of good childhood education programs do not "fade-out" but rather continue to provide benefits for the child throughout their academic career and professional attainment. [52]

The Federal Reserve of Chicago's research shows that upward economic mobility has declined since 1980, largely due to factors like stagnant wages, increased consumption inequality, and the rising income share of the top 1%.[53] Addressing economic mobility requires investment in education, particularly early childhood programs, which play a significant role but are not a cure-all.

From inception to now reality, the Discovery Cube in Sylmar, Los Angeles, illustrates how community commitment and visionary leadership can create impactful educational opportunities—its programs have reached over 69,000 children.

When I began working with California State Assemblymember Tony Cardenas in 1997, I didn't know the term "economic mobility," but quickly learned how policy influences opportunity. Just as policies once limited economic mobility, new policies can foster it for future generations, as seen in initiatives like Communities in Schools. The mission of Communities in Schools is simple; it is to keep children in school.[54]

As I have mentioned, there is plenty of research supporting the correlation between academic access/success and an individual's ability to build wealth as an adult. In the Federal Reserve of St. Louis' work *Education, Income and Wealth*, they found that when they compared people with more and less education, oftentimes those with more education earn greater incomes and are unemployed less than those with less education.[55] I have no doubt that the Assembly Member knew the importance of education in a person's life and the impact it would have on a person's ability to provide for themselves and their families.

Growing up in a humble household of immigrants, he

lived in a community rich in culture and community but one that lacked economic opportunity. Some of his neighbors knew all too well that their children were not going to school but rather were caught up in the criminal system. In the Congressman's work, *The Second Chance for Justice*, he highlights the 2019 data around incarceration.[56] In this document, the data highlights that over 696,600 youth under the age of 18 were arrested in the United States. What is even more important in this economic mobility conversation is that 67% of those children arrested are children of color. The research also showed that children of color are also disproportionately transferred to the adult criminal justice system, where they are tried and prosecuted as adults. Lastly, the data showed that Black children are 2.5 times more likely to be arrested than white children.[57]

Addressing economic mobility necessitates a discussion about incarcerated individuals, who represent an important part of our future community. It is essential that, as a society, we support their successful reintegration so they can reach their full potential. Among numerous initiatives championed by the Congressman, he has consistently recognized the critical role of education in this process.

It's worth emphasizing that policy is one of the most influential factors in boosting a city's economic mobility. Thoughtfully crafted and effectively implemented policies can shape the trajectory of entire communities, opening doors to opportunity and fostering environments where individuals and families can thrive. I am convinced that by steadfastly supporting every program and initiative we have developed, we build momentum toward the change we all want to see.

This cumulative effort is not just about incremental progress—it's about creating a world where everyone has equal opportunities to pursue and achieve their own version of greatness. When policies are designed with equity at their core and backed by sustained commitment, they empower both individuals and communities to overcome barriers, realize their potential, and contribute meaningfully to society.

Ultimately, the goal is to ensure that opportunity is not reserved for a select few but is accessible to all. By aligning our actions, resources, and vision, we can foster a future in which every person—regardless of background—has the chance to succeed and shape their own path to greatness.

Scaling Innovation for All: California's Equity-Focused Ecosystem

Over the years, I have dedicated myself to studying innovation and entrepreneurship. My 2011 dissertation focused specifically on whether state energy-efficiency policies influence innovation. Through my research, I discovered that California's policies encouraged manufacturers to achieve greater energy efficiency, unlike those changes driven solely by market forces. The effectiveness of these policies relied on advancements in technology, design, and reduced production costs, demonstrating how targeted policy interventions can accelerate progress beyond what market dynamics alone might achieve.

This research sparked my curiosity about the broader landscape of innovation across California. The state undeniably leads the nation in innovative thinking, but this creativity is not evenly distributed; rather, it is concentrated in distinct regions —especially Sacramento, San Francisco/Bay Area/Silicon Valley, Los Angeles/Orange County, and San Diego. These clusters have become epicenters for technological advancement, entrepreneurship, and economic growth, each benefiting from a unique combination of talent, investment, infrastructure, and supportive policy environments.

California's experience illustrates the powerful interplay between public policy and private sector innovation. By fostering environments that reward efficiency and creativity, the state has set a benchmark for others to follow. The lessons learned from California's approach continue to inform my perspective on how strategic policy decisions can drive meaningful change, encourage regional specialization, and support the development of vibrant innovation ecosystems.

Understanding venture capital is not the sole measure of innovation, but it does provide insight as to where innovation is occurring and being funded. Although California saw a decrease in 2022, as noted by Crunchbase News, California companies still lead with a venture capital investment of $91.9 billion in 4,296 deals.[58] As a result, since February 2021, the State's innovation economy has created nearly 1 million jobs and nearly 16% of the country's new business starts.[59]

The innovation ecosystem significantly influences the state; however, not all communities are reaping its benefits equally. It is evident that effective innovation ecosystems are distinctive and require collaboration among a variety of entities, including educational research institutions, businesses, funding sources, and a robust business sector. A key consideration remains: how can the impact of regional innovation hubs be expanded so that additional communities may experience associated advantages? Is this a feasible objective?

During my tenure with the State of California, we directly addressed this challenge. In partnership with Secretary of Business, Transportation and Housing, Dale Bonner and Deputy Secretary Brian McGown, the iHub Program was established. Launched in 2010, the iHub Program aimed to enhance accessibility to the state's innovation ecosystem, thereby fostering increased employment and investment opportunities for all Californians. The program started with 10 iHubs and eventually grew to 12 iHub communities under this first phase of the program.[60]

This initiative is noteworthy for capitalizing on the State's established reputation for innovation and using that strength to foster greater inclusivity. The objective was to expand access across various communities, enabling them to share in the resulting advantages. It serves as an example of how scaling successful strategies can extend benefits to a broader population.

Within the sphere of economic mobility, such initiatives represent clear opportunities for impactful progress. While developing these programs requires substantial time and effort, the distinctive contributions California offers as a State are widely recognized and undisputed.

The iHub program has now grown into iHub² with a deliberate and intentional mission that focuses "on diversity, equity, and inclusion. The program will accelerate technology and science-based firms in key industry areas with a strong outreach focus on diverse founders, including women and people of color, and underserved geographies and regions."[61]

From Vision to Impact: Scaling Equity Through Federal Innovation Programs

When I was about 16, I took a picture in front of the White House during a trip to D.C. for a CIA internship interview—an opportunity I didn't get. That day, I made a promise to myself that one day I would work in the big White House. Years later, I fulfilled that dream as a Special Assistant in the U.S. Department of Commerce's Economic Development Agency. The job felt surreal; although I did not work in the White House, I was across literarily across the street. Truly, I never quite got used to walking the same halls as our nation's founders or discussing the country's national competitiveness. Commuting into the city never lost its thrill for me, with the Washington Monument, the Mall, and the White House always reminding me of my purpose – my passion. Although my time there was brief, representing the Agency nationwide and at the OECD remains a highlight of my career.

While at the U.S. EDA, both the Assistant Secretary and the Under Secretary wanted to try something new. They wanted to promote a new innovative program but were not quite sure how to launch it. I believe it was the Brian McGowan, the Under Secretary, who suggested a pilot program. By establishing the effort as a 'pilot' it would allow for the agency to pivot to ensure success. It worked!

The first *i6 Challenge* launched in 2010 as a pilot program to support the Regional Innovation Strategies program. To drive support for the Startup America Initiative, the i6 Challenge was created to be a national competition based on the most impactful national models for startup creation, innovation and commercialization.[62] These programs would compete for the $8 million available. Looking back, what was also very important and now would herald as a strong equity program, was that the program specifically called out $2.5 million for rural communities to "promote and support inclusion".[63]

What started out as a pilot program has continued to be successful today. In fact, in 2020 the program received $22 million to disburse throughout the nation. Interestingly, the U.S. EDA published the impact of the *i6 Challenge* program during the 2014-March 2018 programs and the numbers speak for themselves. Throughout this time, *i6 Challenge* made $42 million in awards, which were leveraged/matched with $54 million for a total program spend of just under $1 billion dollars. These funds went to 88 projects in 36 states to support over 4,150 entrepreneurs and startups. These businesses, in return, created and/or retained over 7,160 jobs, raised more than $941 million in capital, and held or had applications in for 1,100 patents.[64] What started out as a pilot program to drive innovation throughout the entire nation has turned out to be a very successful, sustainable national program that has had a true impact.

A key takeaway is that economic mobility programs often originate from bold, unconventional ideas and require a willingness to take risks. Yet, the political environment frequently leans toward caution and risk aversion. In these situations, launching pilot programs can be particularly effective—they allow organizations to test new strategies on a small scale with limited exposure. If a pilot program does not yield the desired results, it can be discontinued with minimal consequence. However, if it proves successful, the initiative can be scaled up and developed into a mature program, potentially generating long-term, transformative impact.

When Urgency Matters: Equity and Accountability After Deepwater Horizon

A commitment to equity reflects a dedication to fostering a supportive and inclusive community—one that encompasses colleagues, family members, and neighbors. This principle was especially evident during my tenure with the U.S. Department of Commerce, Economic Development Administration (EDA), where I collaborated with teams organizing federal delegations to coastal communities in Louisiana, Alabama, and Florida affected by the 2010 Deepwater Horizon Oil Spill in the Gulf of Mexico. The repercussions of this disaster were severe, with detrimental effects on both the environment and local economies. For regions reliant on tourism and fishing, the impact was exceptionally significant.

Britannica describes the Deepwater Horizon Oil Spill as "the largest marine oil spill in history," noting that petroleum released before the well was sealed resulted in a slick covering over 57,500 square miles. At the incident's height, over one third of federal waters in the gulf were closed to fishing due to contamination concerns.

To address these challenges, federal response teams were deployed to evaluate the extent of the environmental crisis and implement strategies promoting economic recovery for impacted families. Additionally, these teams provided communities with real-time access to specific agency programs, resources, and development opportunities.

At a concluding community meeting in Louisiana, I encountered an individual named Bubba, whose impassioned remarks underscored the urgency felt within his community. Bubba articulated his frustration regarding what he perceived as a slow response in addressing their needs following this unprecedented disaster. He explained how the local economy, largely dependent on fishing and oil industries, had been severely disrupted. Critical ecosystems were compromised, resulting in substantial job losses and hardship for many families. Meaningful support, he noted, appeared delayed, and the path to recovery remained uncertain.

The impact Bubba described was echoed in research by

Columbia University's National Center for Disaster Preparedness. In July 2010, the center conducted more than 1,200 telephone interviews, finding that one in five households reported a drop in income and 8% reported a job loss.[65] The losses were most likely to hit those already economically vulnerable: households with incomes under $25,000 a year. Economically, the situation was dire. Analysts estimated that the Louisiana fishing industry could sustain $2.5 billion in losses, while Florida could lose $3 billion in tourism income.

Bubba was not alone in his ongoing frustration with the federal government's emergency response—first, there was Hurricane Katrina, from which many families had yet to recover, followed by the subsequent oil spill. These events significantly impacted the affected communities, leading many residents to feel abandoned during their recovery process.

The atmosphere in the room was solemn as Bubba expressed his concerns, and the federal team listened intently, recognizing the deep sense of urgency in his remarks. Before addressing the community's pain and loss or initiating plans for economic recovery, it was essential to document the full scope of issues and develop appropriate recommendations. Explaining this necessary, though often complex, process did not provide the reassurance Bubba and the community sought. We acknowledged that their situation required immediate attention and understood that procedural timelines felt inadequate under such circumstances. Bubba concluded his comments by asking me to "read through the lines," emphasizing the need for decisive action.

This moment underscored the widespread distress within these communities, as many did not perceive an adequate sense of urgency from government agencies. Personally, and professionally, I found this experience profoundly challenging. Despite my determination to provide support, the mechanisms available would require weeks to implement.

After the meeting, Bubba approached me, offered an apology, and invited me to his home. He elaborated on his frustration with what he saw as unfulfilled promises from government officials who, after voicing commitment, would return to Washington, D.C., without delivering tangible results for his family and community.

This experience has remained significant to me. Meeting Bubba reinforced the critical importance of timely action and illuminated the genuine consequences of delayed or insufficient responses for those we serve in public administration. While governmental processes and procedures are vital, they can also present perceived obstacles, even when designed to facilitate aid. My interaction with Bubba strengthened my resolve to approach this work with an ongoing sense of urgency and responsiveness.

Although I did not see Bubba again, the lessons learned from our encounter continue to influence my perspective and approach to service.

Harnessing Local Strengths: Development and Preparedness After Disaster

Like many others across the country, I was riveted to the television during Hurricane Maria—a powerful Category 5 storm that devastated Dominica, Martinique, Saint Croix, and Puerto Rico in September 2017. Its aftermath marked it as one of the most catastrophic hurricanes these islands had ever faced, leaving communities grappling with unprecedented destruction and loss. The images of flooded streets, toppled infrastructure, and families struggling to recover were a stark reminder of the vulnerability that so many communities face in the wake of natural disasters.

When the International Economic Development Council called for volunteers to join an economic development recovery team, I eagerly accepted the chance to contribute to the recovery efforts. I felt a deep sense of responsibility to use my experience to support communities in need, knowing that rebuilding after such devastation requires not only resources but also collaboration, empathy, and long-term commitment.

Typically, economic recovery initiatives begin only after the immediate crisis has passed—once basic needs are met and the initial emergency response winds down. This was the case with my journey to Manati, Puerto Rico, which began in April 2019, well after the storm's landfall. My time in Manati reinforced a critical lesson relevant to our work on economic mobility: preparedness is essential. Every community, regardless of size or location, faces risks from both natural and human-made disasters, and we must always be ready to respond and adapt.

This experience underscored the importance of building resilient systems, fostering strong partnerships, and maintaining a proactive approach to community development. By investing in preparedness and recovery planning, we can help ensure that when disaster strikes, communities are not only able to recover but also to emerge stronger and more equitable than before.

Upon arriving, I quickly engaged with the local efforts. My primary contact was in the City of Manati's Office of Federal Affairs, responsible for leading the city's revitalization. Of the nine staff members, my role was part-time and focused on general economic development. The other eight concentrated on leveraging various federal programs, such as Community Development Block Grants, Section 8, and FEMA initiatives. Collaborating with both national and local teams who were already active on the ground, we identified several community priorities. These included establishing a Main Street Program, a Business Improvement District, an artist village, developing federal Opportunity Zones, and expanding the medical tourism sector.

Drawing on research conducted before my arrival, I advised the city to build upon its existing strengths in the medical ecosystem and concentrate on medical tourism. This strategy would not only enhance healthcare access and create jobs but also attract new businesses and investments. Manati was well-positioned for this goal, with robust infrastructure like hospitals, medical offices, technical colleges dedicated to medical training, pharmaceutical companies, and skilled professionals—

all elements conducive to a thriving medical innovation incubator.

My recommendation centered on leveraging and elevating Manati's competitive advantage through the creation of a medical incubator. Such an initiative would meet essential health service needs, stimulate job growth, and encourage further investment, forming a solid foundation for economic mobility. Although I haven't revisited the city since my original engagement, my research revealed that Manati is home to specialized facilities like the Endocrinology Innovation Center and many more.

The cornerstone of effective economic mobility work lies in engaging key stakeholders—they possess invaluable insights into their communities, past efforts, and current needs. By actively involving local leaders, business owners, and residents in the planning and implementation process, organizations can ensure that strategies are grounded in real-world experience and tailored to address genuine challenges.

In the case of Manati, as with other communities, harnessing an existing competitive edge through the lens of economic mobility proved to be mutually beneficial for both the community and the city. By identifying and leveraging local strengths—such as established industries, unique cultural assets, or specialized workforce skills—stakeholders were able to collaborate on initiatives that not only addressed immediate recovery needs but also laid the foundation for long-term growth and resilience.

This approach demonstrates that sustainable economic mobility is most successful when it builds upon the assets and aspirations of the community itself. When stakeholders are empowered to contribute their expertise and vision, the resulting programs are more likely to gain traction, foster trust, and deliver meaningful impact.

Building Pathways: Personal Perseverance and Strategic Partnerships

My mother has always demonstrated remarkable intellect. She never questioned me about whether I would attend college, but rather the question was also which institution I would ultimately choose. From an early age, post-secondary education was presented to me not as an option, but as a natural progression, similar to advancing between primary school grades. Despite neither of my parents having attended college, they were steadfast in providing opportunities for me, regardless of the sacrifices required. For this unwavering support, I remain deeply appreciative. My pursuit of a doctorate became a tribute to their determination as much as my own ambitions.

In preparation for doctoral studies, I recognized the necessity of pursuing a master's degree. UCLA was a logical choice due to its proximity to my workplace and longstanding reputation. Having previously been accepted for undergraduate studies, I anticipated admission would be straightforward; however, I was disheartened by a rejection letter. In hindsight, I believe such setbacks serve a purpose. My mother, recognizing my disappointment, encouraged resilience and proactive action.

Despite initially seeking comfort, I followed her advice and devised a strategy to gain admission. I audited two courses within the master's program and excelled academically. Fortuitously, one audited course was led by the chair of the admissions committee. Earning a high grade, securing a recommendation letter from him, and participating actively in office hours proved instrumental in my eventual acceptance to the program.

The three years devoted to the Urban Planning and Latin American Affairs master's program at UCLA were foundational for my subsequent work in economic development. The curriculum shaped my strategic approach to urban policy and community advancement. Notably, Dr. Raul Hinojosa, recognized for his expertise in US-Mexico-Latin America trade and migration relations, was among my professors. His commitment to the field was evident and influential.

Through Dr. Hinojosa's mentorship, I gained valuable connections. While serving as District Director for City Council

Member Alex Padilla, I engaged in numerous discussions about municipal strategies. This culminated in an introduction to Dr. Juan Hernandez, who, in collaboration with Mexican President Vicente Fox, established the Office of External Affairs—the first such entity dedicated to promoting small businesses across the US-Mexico border. Leading this initiative, Dr. Hernandez fostered cross-border commercial relationships, a significant strategic development given the substantial economic impact documented in both nations.

In 2021, the Pew Research Center found that there are about 37.2 million people of Mexican origin living in the United States, which represents almost 60% of the nation's total U.S. Hispanic population.[66] Additionally, Mexico has become very dependent on the remittances it receives from Mexicans in the United States sending funds to their families in Mexico. The Federal Reserve of Dallas reports that $41 billion was sent in 2020.[67] To put this in perspective, remittances surpass tourism, oil exports and most manufacturing exports as a source of the country's foreign income.[68] In fact, if we look at remittances as a percentage of Mexico's GDP it represented 3.8% in 2020.[69] Finally, the U.S. Department of State reported that in 2021, the U.S. goods and services trade with Mexico totaled $725.7 billion that makes Mexico the United States' second largest trading partner. Considering the economic development impact, in 2019, the U.S. exports of goods and services to Mexico supported an estimated 1.1 million jobs.[70] For all these reasons, this office made sense.

During the meeting, I observed attentively as an invited guest of Dr. Hinojosa. At one point, Dr. Hinojosa asked me to describe my role supporting the Council Member, which I was pleased to do. I outlined our strategic approach to establishing the office for the newly elected Council Member. Anticipating that Dr. Hernandez might prefer another topic, I then discussed the economic impact of trade between the U.S. and Mexico. Contrary to my expectations, Dr. Hernandez expressed continued interest in the systems implemented for constituent service and business operations, prompting me to further elaborate on both areas. This conversation marked the beginning of an ongoing dialogue with Dr. Hernandez, who was concurrently organizing his new office and appreciated our district's constituent service model as it aligned with his goal of strengthening representation for businesses and communities.

Acknowledging that the Mexican Consulates offer additional channels for public engagement, I viewed our strategy as a complementary resource. Subsequently, Dr. Hernandez invited me to Los Pinos to present the constituent service tool to his team. It was an honor to contribute to this work and collaborate with the President and staff. Ultimately, the office developed a system designed to monitor constituent and business requests, aiming to deliver superior customer service and facilitate effective commercial and diplomatic interactions.

In the context of economic mobility initiatives, it is crucial to implement mechanisms that enable community members and businesses to express their concerns and ideas. Establishing open channels for feedback—such as community forums, surveys, or advisory groups—not only empowers stakeholders but also ensures that programs remain responsive to real needs.

Equally important is the emphasis on robust data collection. Thoughtfully designed systems for gathering and analyzing data provide the metrics necessary for measuring outcomes, tracking progress, and confirming impact. These insights allow organizations to make informed adjustments, demonstrate accountability, and communicate results transparently to all stakeholders.

By combining inclusive engagement with data-driven strategies, communities can ensure that economic mobility efforts are both meaningful and measurable. This thoughtful approach lays the foundation for sustained progress in community and business development.

Key Takeaways for Part 3: Equity-Focused Case Studies

The case studies presented in this section collectively demonstrate the transformative potential of intentional, data-driven, and collaborative approaches in advancing equity and economic mobility across a wide range of communities. Each example underscores how strategic planning, rigorous analysis, and partnership among stakeholders can address complex challenges and foster sustainable progress.

While every case study could merit an in-depth exploration on its own, the purpose of this section is to distill the most salient lessons and actionable insights. By highlighting key thematic areas—such as stakeholder engagement, evidence-based decision making, and adaptive program design—this section aims to provide practitioners and policymakers with a practical framework for developing and implementing effective equity strategies.

These real-world examples illustrate that successful equity initiatives are not the result of isolated efforts but rather emerge from coordinated actions that leverage local strengths, prioritize inclusivity, and remain responsive to evolving community needs. The strategies and best practices outlined here are intended to serve as a foundation for those seeking to design, launch, or refine programs that drive meaningful and measurable change.

While each example is shaped by its unique context, several core themes and strategies consistently emerge:

1. Data-Driven Decision Making
    - Atlanta's Neighborhood Equity Index: Used 26 indicators to identify and prioritize disinvested neighborhoods for targeted investment and support, ensuring resources reached those most in need.
    - Equity-Based Scoring: Grant and loan programs incorporated equity metrics, such as location, race, and gender, to ensure fair access and outcomes for small businesses in underserved areas.
2. Intentional Policy and Program Design

- Tax Increment Financing (TADs): Invest Atlanta re-evaluated program criteria to remove barriers for minority developers, introduced pre-development loans, and provided technical support, increasing participation and impact in historically marginalized neighborhoods.
- E3 Matrix for Business Attraction: Companies seeking incentives in Atlanta must commit to equity goals, such as fair wages, benefits, and partnerships with nonprofits, embedding equity into economic development strategy.
- Owner-Occupied Rehabilitation: Targeted interventions, informed by stakeholder feedback and data-driven analysis, can significantly advance service delivery, equity and resilience within communities.

3. Collaborative Partnerships

- Food Desert Initiatives: Atlanta's municipal grocery stores and food access programs were made possible by partnerships with city leadership, MARTA, Georgia Tech, Atlanta Food Bank, Goodr, Urban Farmers, and local grocers, demonstrating the power of cross-sector collaboration.
- San Bernardino County: Equity strategies were supported by comprehensive marketing and engagement with a wide range of partners, emphasizing transparency and shared responsibility.

4. Community Engagement and Empowerment

- Los Angeles: Community listening sessions, brainstorming, and prioritizing "low-hanging fruit" fostered trust and momentum. Programs like Discovery Cube and Communities in Schools were shaped by direct input from residents and local leaders.
- Mexico: Constituent service models and open feedback channels ensured that economic mobility initiatives responded to real community needs.

5. Innovation and Adaptability

- California's iHub Program: Expanded access to innovation ecosystems by intentionally including diverse founders and underserved regions, showing how policy can drive inclusion and regional specialization.
- U.S. Economic Development Agency's i6 Challenge: Piloted bold, unconventional ideas, with successful programs scaled nationally to support entrepreneurs and rural inclusion.

6. Resilience and Preparedness

- Puerto Rico: Post-disaster recovery in Manati highlighted the importance of preparedness, leveraging local strengths, and engaging stakeholders to build resilient systems and foster long-term growth.

Common Threads Across All Case Studies

- Equity is embedded in every stage—from policy design and resource allocation to implementation and evaluation.
- Data and metrics guide decisions, ensuring transparency and accountability.
- Collaboration is essential, bringing together government, nonprofits, businesses, and residents.
- Community voices shape solutions, making programs relevant and sustainable.
- Innovation and flexibility allow for adaptation to local context and changing needs.
- Focus on long-term impact, not just immediate relief, drives systemic change.

The Equity Blueprint's case studies demonstrate that advancing equity is a dynamic, ongoing process. Success depends on intentional strategies, robust data, inclusive engagement, and strong partnerships. By integrating these strategies, organizations and communities can create pathways to opportunity and foster sustainable, inclusive growth.

PART IV:

A PERSONAL PATH TOWARD EQUITY

My Path to Community and Economic Development

Like many, I didn't set out to join this field—I stumbled upon it after my employer wouldn't allow me to pursue a master's in urban planning at UCLA because daytime study was against their policy. My interest in planning stemmed from a desire to work in government, believing it would enable me to make a real difference in communities. I recall my high school teacher, Mrs. Diegas, asking what I wanted to be; although I was unsure at the time, I knew I loved travel, languages, and I had a passion to make a positive impact on the world.

This early curiosity about the world and commitment to service became the foundation for my career. The path was not linear, but each unexpected turn—whether a closed door or a new opportunity—helped shape my understanding of how thoughtful planning and public service can transform communities. Looking back, I realize that the drive to create meaningful change has always guided my choices, even when the destination was unclear.

Supported by my husband, I left my job to return to

school, driven by the firm belief—instilled by my parents, who valued education as life's great equalizer—that furthering my studies would build my skills to impact the better future. My mother always reminded me that no one could take away my education or experiences. As a first-generation American, this perspective made me see education as the key to opportunity.

Handing in my resignation was not easy but I knew it was the right thing to do. As I began the transition out of the company, one call changed my life. Rick, with Assemblyman Tony Cardenas's office, open the door to an unexpected job interview with then Chief of Staff Alex Padilla and ultimately with Assemblyman Cardenas himself. Though I had no political background, I leveraged my private sector experience and landed a part-time Constituent Case Manager job.

My first task was constituent requests—a vital role in any government office. It taught me crucial lessons in community engagement and clear communication, both highly valued by Assemblyman Cardenas. As a member of the team, I staffed the Assemblyman at various events and became completely committed to the work as his story and passion were contagious. At the core, his speech was about equity, access, the right to pursue your dreams by working hard.

Things became even more interesting when Alex Padilla ran for Los Angeles City Council, and I supported his underdog campaign. Despite challenging odds, our team's dedication paid off, and Alex became the youngest council member for District 7. He soon appointed me District Director, and on my first day, I was tasked with creating a small business strategy. Lacking direct experience, I decided to walk Pacoima's Van Nuys Boulevard, talking to as many small business owners as possible. Their input shaped our business outreach platform and taught me the importance of listening instead of assuming.

This formative experience provided me with a path to pursuing my dream of moving the needle in community through economic and community development strategies. Since then, I've had the opportunity to work across a wide spectrum of areas—including commercial corridors, international trade, tourism, incentives, disaster recovery, innovation, affordable housing, workforce programs, and small business loans.

What I've learned is that economic and community development is not just about jobs and investment. It's about shaping the very fabric of community life—encompassing everything from housing and entertainment to arts and culture. Each project, whether focused on revitalizing a neighborhood, supporting entrepreneurs, or expanding access to affordable housing, contributes to building vibrant, resilient communities where people can thrive.

This holistic approach has shown me that true progress is achieved when we address the interconnected needs of individuals, small businesses and neighborhoods, and when we recognize that economic and community development touches every aspect of daily life.

All these diverse experiences have brought me to where I am today. The beauty of this work is its variety—there is no typical day, and the roles available are many. Universities, hospitals, nonprofits, small businesses, and cultural institutions all play a part, and creating vibrant places requires involvement from every sector of the community.

It is this diversity of people, perspectives, and partnerships that makes economic and community development so rewarding. Each day brings new challenges and opportunities, and the collective effort of stakeholders across sectors is what truly shapes thriving, resilient communities.

My Personal Journey

Throughout my career, I have had the privilege of working in diverse regions—from Los Angeles and San Bernardino in California to Washington D.C. and Atlanta. My professional path has also included advising the Mexican government and supporting city recovery efforts in Puerto Rico. Across these varied experiences, one constant has emerged: underserved communities consistently face the greatest challenges, particularly in relation to poverty and chronic underinvestment.

These neighborhoods have always held a special significance for me, perhaps because they evoke memories of my own upbringing. I grew up in Rosemead, California, a modest working-class city. I recall hearing it described as being on "the wrong side of the tracks," a phrase that, at the time, held little meaning for me. To me, Rosemead was simply home—a place whose affordability made it accessible for many Latino families like mine.

My family's story is one of resilience and determination. Both of my parents were immigrants: my mother from Mexico and my father from what was then Yugoslavia (Serbia). My father's early life was marked by profound hardship, shaped by the aftermath of World War II. As a child, he was sent to a labor camp with his mother and grandmother, enduring years of forced labor. He rarely spoke of those experiences, but when he did, his emotions were palpable. With the help of an aunt, he eventually escaped after losing both his mother and grandmother. Thanks to the Red Cross, he made his way to the United States at age sixteen.

After settling in Los Angeles, my father discovered his talent as a mechanic. Through tireless work—seven days a week—he eventually opened his own body shop, "There Is A Difference." It became a family enterprise, with my mother managing the accounts and my siblings and I contributing as assistants, apprentices, and receptionists. The daily commute to the shop provided cherished moments with my father, who imparted wisdom that has guided me throughout my life. One lesson stands out: "nothing lasts forever." He lived by this principle, embracing life fully despite adversity. His empathy and generosity left a lasting impact, not only on our family but on countless others whose lives he touched.

My mother's journey was equally remarkable. Before meeting my father, she was a single parent fleeing an abusive relationship in Mexico, seeking safety and opportunity in Los Angeles. She found shelter with a friend who would later become her mother-in-law, illustrating the unexpected ways families can form and grow. In other words, my mother's best friend married Jozef, and she herself married his son, Frank, intertwining their lives and cultures even further.

This tapestry of backgrounds and experiences is, to me, emblematic of what makes America unique: people from different origins coming together to build families that blend cultures, languages, and traditions—united by love, hard work, and perseverance.

As a child, I visited my great-grandmother in Mexico, whose humble adobe house had dirt floors she kept immaculate. She welcomed us with warmth, and I still remember the taste of her handmade tortillas and fresh beans. My mother instilled in me the importance of respecting and valuing everyone, regardless of their circumstances—a lesson that has shaped my worldview and commitment to equity.

My parents raised five children—four boys and me, the youngest and only girl. For them, the American Dream meant safety, peace, and opportunity. They believed in working hard to secure a better future for the entire family. Our immigrant roots taught us to appreciate the opportunities America offered, and to approach life with determination, grit, and unwavering commitment.

Inspired by my parents' unwavering dedication to hard work, compassion, and the pursuit of a better life—not only for themselves, but for others—I have embraced a lifelong commitment to advancing equity and driving meaningful change in communities everywhere. Their resilience in the face of adversity and their sacrifices have instilled in me a profound sense of responsibility to stand up for what I believe in. This book is born from that conviction: equity is not a fleeting ideal or a passing trend—it is a fundamental principle that demands purposeful, sustained action. My purpose in writing this book is to challenge the status quo, illuminate the realities of inequity, and empower others to join in the deliberate work of building a more just and inclusive society.

I believe we cannot afford to treat equity as an abstract concept or allow it to be dismissed as "false news." The persistent disparities in our communities call for more than words; they require each of us to act with purpose and urgency. My hope is that this book will not only illuminate the realities of inequity, but also inspire you—whether as a leader, practitioner, philanthropic investor or neighbor—to join in the deliberate work of building a more just and inclusive society. The time to act is now. Together, we can transform conviction into collective progress and ensure that opportunity is truly accessible to all.

Concluding Thoughts on Advancing Equitable Communities

The central objective of this book is to advance the development of strong, equitable communities by providing a comprehensive blueprint for practitioners, policymakers, and leaders focused on economic and community development. Achieving equity at scale is a complex undertaking, requiring not only the creation but also the sustained implementation of programs that address disparities across entire communities and regions. Drawing upon years of experience collaborating with diverse constituencies, I have endeavored to distill actionable insights and present practical recommendations that can drive long-term, systemic impact.

While many of the concepts and strategies discussed herein are not novel, the value of this work lies in its synthesis—bringing together proven approaches, lessons learned, and real-world case studies in a single resource. My hope is that these examples will inspire readers to adapt and innovate, creating programs tailored to the unique needs and aspirations of their own communities.

Each year, my family sets intentional goals, and for the past four years, authoring this book has been among my highest priorities. My aim is to offer meaningful guidance to colleagues, professionals and friends who are committed to enhancing community outcomes through the lens of equitable economic mobility. This resource is designed to bridge the gap between theory and practice, equipping practitioners with the tools and perspectives necessary to translate vision into action.

Despite a robust body of literature examining income inequality and its disproportionate effects on communities of color and other marginalized groups, there remains a notable gap in the field regarding effective implementation. To address this, I have compiled a diverse array of information, narratives, and programmatic strategies that have demonstrated measurable success. The intention is to share best practices and motivate those working in economic and community development to advance equity in their own contexts.

The case studies presented throughout this book illustrate a range of approaches for initiating change within communities. It is important to emphasize that there is no universal solution; progress is achieved through a combination of innovative, targeted, and sustained efforts. Furthermore, it is essential to recognize that longstanding policies have contributed to persistent inequities, and reversing these effects will require ongoing commitment and perseverance.

Every strategy implemented to address inequality yields incremental progress. With this in mind, I introduce the Equity at Scale (EaS) model—a framework designed to operationalize equity initiatives and support a community's economic mobility strategies. This work demands optimism, adaptability, and a relentless focus on identifying and leveraging opportunities for improvement. As my grandmother wisely stated, "positive attracts positive." While challenges and setbacks are inevitable, lasting change is built upon resilience, collaboration, and a willingness to learn from experience.

Ultimately, those engaged in economic development are united by a desire to effect positive change and leave the world better than they found it. By cultivating strategic partnerships and connecting with others who share this vision, we can collectively advance our mission to enhance community well-being, both now and in the future. The journey toward equity is a shared endeavor, and finding allies who are equally dedicated to this work is essential for sustained progress.

As you develop and implement strategies to foster greater equity in your communities, I extend my best wishes for your success. My hope is that, as these efforts flourish, resources such as this book will one day become unnecessary—having fulfilled their purpose in helping to move the needle toward a more just and inclusive society.

CHAPTER SUMMARIES

In an effort to spark curiosity and motivate readers to dive deeper into specific chapters, especially those that address their personal or professional challenges; as well as in an effort to help the reader understand the overall structure and progression of the book, so they know what to expect and can navigate to sections most relevant to their interests, I have provided the following chapter summaries.

Part I: Understanding Equity

Sets the stage by exploring the persistent challenge of inequity in the United States, tracing its historical roots, and highlighting the need for deliberate, collaborative action to close opportunity gaps. Readers are invited to reflect on the legacy of inequity and the urgency of designing effective solutions.

Part II: Meeting People Where They Are

Delves into the practical realities of designing equity-focused programs that serve both individuals and entire communities. This section moves beyond theory, offering actionable guidance for practitioners, policymakers, and leaders who want to drive measurable change.

1. Balancing Individual and Community Needs

The section emphasizes that effective equity work requires a dual focus: meeting the unique needs of individuals while also achieving scalable impact across communities. Programs must be flexible enough to provide tailored support, yet robust enough to address systemic challenges.

2. Intentional Outreach

Outreach is not a one-size-fits-all endeavor. The book highlights the importance of understanding the target audience —whether seniors, business owners, or marginalized groups— and using creative, multi-channel strategies to engage them. Examples include attending community events, offering support in multiple languages, and leveraging both digital and in-person methods to ensure accessibility.

3. Problem Identification

Practitioners are encouraged to start by acknowledging the existence of inequities, listening to diverse perspectives, and using data to uncover hidden barriers. The process involves honest conversations, community feedback, and a willingness to challenge assumptions about what works.

4. Program Evaluation and Adaptation

Continuous evaluation is vital. The book advocates for humility and openness to change, recognizing that programs must evolve as communities do. Regular assessment, stakeholder feedback, and external reviews help organizations identify what's effective and where improvements are needed.

5. Openness to Innovation

Innovation is framed as essential for equity work. Leaders are urged to embrace new tools, approaches, and partnerships, and to foster environments where experimentation and learning from failure are encouraged. Cross-sector collaboration and shared learning are highlighted as drivers of sustainable solutions.

6. The Critical Role of Data

Data is presented as a cornerstone for equity. It enables organizations to set benchmarks, measure progress, and hold themselves accountable. The section discusses the importance of combining quantitative metrics with qualitative stories, using both lagging and leading indicators, and ensuring data is accessible and actionable for all stakeholders.

7. Stakeholder Engagement

Engaging stakeholders—residents, businesses, nonprofits, and government agencies—is central to advancing equity. The book provides strategies for building trust, fostering consensus, and ensuring that all voices are included in decision-making processes.

8. Measuring Progress in Real Time

The section encourages practitioners to use real-time feedback and adaptive management to refine programs. Transparent reporting, regular check-ins, and the use of technology for continuous engagement are recommended to keep initiatives relevant and effective.

Practical Takeaways

Design with empathy: Understand the lived experiences of those you serve.

Iterate and improve: Treat every program as a work in progress, open to refinement.

Leverage partnerships: Collaborate across sectors to maximize resources and impact.

Use data wisely: Combine hard numbers with human stories to drive change.

Empower communities: Make engagement and feedback central to every initiative.

Part III: The Equity Blueprint, Case Studies

Presents real-world examples and best practices from Atlanta, Los Angeles, California, Puerto Rico, and beyond. Each case study illustrates how intentional strategies, data-driven decision-making, and cross-sector partnerships can address issues such as food deserts, housing stability, small business support, disaster recovery, and more. The section emphasizes adaptability, collaboration, and community engagement as keys to achieving lasting change, and provides actionable insights for practitioners.

Part IV: A Personal Path Toward Equity

Shares my personal journey, shaped by family resilience, immigrant experience, and a commitment to service. This section reflects on lessons learned from diverse regions and roles, showing how these experiences inform a holistic approach to economic and community development. The author concludes with a call to action, inviting readers to join in building more just and inclusive communities through purposeful, sustained effort.

GRAPHS, CHARTS, FIGURES

GC-1
INVEST ATLANTA SCORING MATRIX

1. Located in an ARP-designated Qualified Census Tract

10 points if applicant is located in a Qualified Census Tract.

2. Located in a Federal Opportunity Zone

10 points if applicant is located in a Federal Opportunity Zone.

3. Located in disinvested NPU's

5 points if applicant is located in disinvested NPU

4. Located in Tax Allocation District (TAD) or City of Atlanta designated Redev. Area

5 points if applicant is located in a TAD or Redevelopment Area

5. Veteran owned business

5 points if applicant is a veteran owned business

6. Business certified as one or more of the following by the city, GDOT and/or MARTA.

• Min Bus. Enterprise, Female Bus. Enterprise, Small Bus. Enterprise, Disadvantaged Bus Enterprise

10 points if applicant is certified as one or more of the above.

7. Did not receive previous round of Resurgence funding or other Grant funds

10 points if applicant didn't receive previous grant funds 8 points if received $0 - $50,000

5 points if received $50,000 - $100,000

1 point if received $100,001+

8. Assess the impact of the COVID-19 on the business.

9. Assess impact of awarded funds for business' plans for re-opening and/or adaption to a post-COVID environment.

GC-2

E3 Partnership Development Worksheet

Economic Opportunity Fund Tier Requirements:

Tier 1 - If the offered grant is greater than $500,000, select at least 10 commitments below

Tier 2 - If the offered grant is between $250,000 and $500,000, select at least 8 commitments below

Tier 3 - If the offered grant is between $100,000 and $250,000, select at least 6 commitments below

Tier 4 - If the offered grant is less than $100,000, select at least 4 commitments:

HIRING PRACTICES

Hire at least ____ (depending on size of project) employees through WorkSource Atlanta into living wage jobs

Enact or continue "second chance" hiring practices

Recruit ____ homeless, veterans and/or disabled City of Atlanta residents

Not require compulsory pre-employment drug screening for prospective employees in non-safety sensitive positions

EMPLOYEE BENEFITS

Provide a minimum of twelve weeks paid family leave for all employees

Offer and partially pay for health insurance benefits to partners and dependents of employees who receive insurance benefits

Offer corporate sponsored Health Savings Plans

Provide corporate sponsored life insurance policies for all employees

Offer on-site, corporate sponsored childcare or childcare vouchers covering 50% of childcare costs for employees

Pay (fully or at least 50% subsidized) and provide time for study and/or class participation for college and technical college education

Provide workforce training/career pathways for at least ____ low wage (~$40k) workers

Offer or lead/participate in an employer assisted housing program (employer-offered down-payment or rental subsidy), either homeownership, rental, or both for employees

Provide employees with a commuting allowance of $50.00 stipend per month to offset public transit costs and participation with other shared vehicle options.

CORPORATE COMMITMENT TO EQUITY

Create and/or maintain a robust corporate diversity policy with at least 15% minority and women owned business purchasing participation

Maintain ____ % of minority, women, and underrepresented groups on the company's corporate board

Require yearly Diversity and Inclusion/Unconscious Bias training for all employees

Create/maintain an internal mentorship program for women/employees of color and underrepresented groups

EDUCATIONAL PARTNERSHIPS

Partner with APS to provide ____ mentorships, internships, and/or youth employment opportunities to students from underrepresented communities

Join, create, or sponsor an "Adopt a School or Cluster" program with an APS within a Disinvested Neighborhoods or at least 50% participation in free/reduced lunch programs

Partner with a local organization and education institutions to provide(s) ____ paid internship/apprenticeship/workplace learning programs for City of Atlanta residents

Provide a corporate level sponsorship of an extracurricular activity program at an Atlanta Public School and/or Atlanta Partners for Education (sports teams, computer clubs, debate clubs, chorus/band/orchestra, community service organizations)

Partner with a HBCU or another education institution to provide ____ paid internship/ work study opportunities for students including company mentorship

ADVANCING OPPORTUNITIES FOR ATLANTANS

Partner/Support a local nonprofit by investing in their success (i.e.: donation, in-kind services, etc.) as the nonprofit is making a difference in the lives of Atlantans on a yearly basis

Meaningfully engage/support Atlanta's non-profit ecosystem through volunteerism, philanthropy, advocacy, and other corporate social responsibility efforts

Partner/Support nonprofit cultural institutions whose mission is to advance culture and arts in the city with a donation, in-kind, services, etc.

Partner/Support nonprofits within Disinvested Neighborhoods who are making a difference in the community

Engage in recruitment efforts for Atlantans living within Disinvested Neighborhoods throughout the City.

Join and meaningfully engage in peer-to-peer events, small business mentorship, and other initiatives to grow industry clusters and make them more accessible to minorities, women, and other underrepresented groups

Commit to sourcing equipment, supplies, and improvements from existing small businesses based/headquartered in the City of Atlanta;

Figures

BIBLIOGRAPHY

Bailey, Jay. https://russellcenter.org/about-us/ Retrieved November 8, 2025.

n.d. *About The King Center.* Accessed December 15, 2022. www.thekingcenter.org.

Associated Press. 2023. "Money Mexican Migrants Send Home Up 13.4% in 2022." *Associated Press*, February 1.

Belsky, Eric. 2018. "Lack of Access to Financial Services Impedes Economic Mobility." *Federal Reserve Bank of Atlanta.* October 16. Accessed February 12, 2023. https://www.atlantafed.org/economy-matters/community-and-economic-development/2018/10/16/lack-of-access-to-financial-services-impedes-economic-mobility.

Bennis, W., & Nanus, B. (1985). *Leaders: The strategies for taking charge.* New York: Harper & Row.

Bryant, John Hope. 2022. *How Credit Scores Can Transform a Community* (October 6).

Canas, Jesus, and Chloe Smith. 2021. "Investment in Mexico Falls Despite Rise In Remittances." *Federal Reserve Bank of Dallas.*

Cardenas, Tony, Karen Bass, and Cory Booker. 2019. "Second Chance For Justice Juvenile Justice and Criminal Justice Package." Legislative Package, Sacramento.

Clark, Sarah, and Gary Freed. 2020. "Teen Involvement in Demonstrations Against Police Brutality." *Mott Poll Report* (C.S.

Mott Children's Hospital) 37 (2): 1-2.

Commentary, Guest. 2022. "R&D Investments Drive California Innovation." *Cal Matters.*

Communities in Schools. n.d. *Who We Are.* Accessed September 23, 2023. https://www.cislosangeles.org/mission.html.

Consumer Financial Protection Bureau. 2020. "What Are The Costs and Fees For A Payday Loan?" *Consumer Financial Protection Bureau.* August 28. Accessed October 30, 2023. https://www.consumerfinance.gov/ask-cfpb/what-are-the-costs-and-fees-for-a-payday-loan-en-1589/ .

Deane, Claudia. *Americans Deeping Mistrust of Institutions.* October 17, 2024. https://www.pew.org/en/trend/archive/fall-2024/americans-deepening-mistrust-of-institutions#:~:text=Americans'%20trust%20in%20the%20federal,adequately%20careful%20with%20tax-payer%20money.

Discovery Cube OC & LA. n.d. *Who We Are.* Accessed September 23, 2023. https://www.discoverycube.org/.

Eisenmann, Tom. 2021. "Why Start-Ups Fail." *Harvard Business Review*, May-June.

Farrigan, Tracey. 2021. "Data Show US Poverty Rates in 2019 Higher In Rural Areas Than In Urban For Racial/Ethnic Groups." *Economic Research Service.* August 23. Accessed December 15, 2022. https://www.ers.usda.gov/data-products/chart-gallery/gallery/chart-detail/?chartId=101903#:~:text=Data%20show%20U.S.%20poverty%20rates,urban)%20areas%20at%2011.9%20percent.

Federal Deposit Insurance Corporation, 2023 FDIC National Survey of Unbanked and Underbanked Households. https://www.fdic.gov/household-survey/2023-

fdic-national-survey-unbanked-and-underbanked-house-holds-report

Federal Reserve Bank of St. Louis. n.d. *Education, Income and Wealth (Page One Economics)*. Accessed September 23, 2023. https://www.stlouisfed.org/en/education/page-one-economics-classroom-edition/education-income-and-wealth.

Feldman, Megan. 2018. "New Harvard Study Reveals Lasting Benefits of Quality Early Childhood Education." *First Five Years Fund*, March 23.

Greble, Emily. 2021. *Conflict in Post-War Yugoslavia: The Search for a Narrative.* September 21. Accessed December 14, 2022. www.nationalww2museum.org .

2020. "Growing Apart: A Politcal History of American Inequality." *Differences that Matter.* April 6. Accessed January 12, 2023. www.scalar.usc.edu .

Herrejon, Margarita. 2023. *Equity: Person Centric.* Artist, Atlanta.

Industrial Economic, Inc. 2018. *Evaluating Technical Assistance and Economic Opportunity Outcomes of Community Advantage Pilot Program.* Power Point, Cambridge: Industrial Economics, Inc.

Jackson, Dylan. 2022. "Atlanta Has the Highest Income Inequality in the Nation, Census Data Shows." *Atlanta Journal Constitution*, November 28.

n.d. "Japanese American Incarceration." *The National WWII Museum New Orleans.* Accessed December 15, 2022. https://www.nationalww2museum.org/war/articles/japanese-american-incarceration .

Jarand, Michael, and Kevin Klowden. 2019. "Rebuilding California's Trade Policy Infrastructure." *Milken Institute.* May 12. Accessed October 15, 2023. https://milkeninstitute.org/sites/default/files/reports-pdf/Rebuilding-Californias-Trade-Policy-Infrastructure-FINAL_0.pdf.

Karo, Carolyn and Mueller, Jackson. *Partnership For Lending in Underserved Markets.* September, 2017. https://milkeninstitute.org/sites/default/files/reports-pdf/092617-PLUM-Phase-I-Summary.pdf

King, Martin Luther. 1965. "Sermon." Sermon, Atlanta, GA.

Kristof, Nicholas. 2020. "Pull Yourself Up By Bootstraps? Go Ahead, Try It." *New York Times*, February 19.

krogstad, Jens Manuel, Jeffrey Passel, Mohamad Moslimani, and Luis Noe-Bustamante. 2023. "Key Facts About U.S. Latinos for National Hispanic Heritage Month." *Pew Research Center.*

Krugman, Paul. 2007. "Politics, Policy and Inequality." *Economic Policy Institute.* May 21. Accessed January 15, 2023. www.epi.org.

Massachusetts Institute of Technology. n.d. *Living Wage Calculator.* Accessed March 18, 2023. https://livingwage.mit.edu.

Menasce Horowitz, Juliana, Ruth Igielnik, and Rakesh Kochhar. 2020. "Trends In Income and Wealth Inequality." *Pew Research Center.* January 9. Accessed February 15, 2023. https://www.pewresearch.org/social-trends/2020/01/09/trends-in-income-and-wealth-inequality/.

Metinko, Chris. 2023. "Venture Fall More Than 40% In Hottest States For Funding." *Crunchbase News.*

Mitchell, Leonard, Deepak Bahl, and Nicholas Busalacchi. 2013. *iHub California Innovation Hub.* Report, Sacramento: USC Center for Economic Development on behalf of the U.S. Department of Commerce, Economic Development Administration.

Mazumder. Bhash. *Intergenerational Economic Mobility in the United States*. Policy Brief, April 2022. Chicago Federal Reserve. https://www.chicagofed.org/research/content-areas/mobility/intergenerational-economic-mobility#:~:text=In%20more%20recent%20work%2C%20my,down ward%20mobility%20from%20the%20top.

"Oil Spill Has Far-Reaching Effects on Children and Families", Columbia University. August 3, 2010 https://www.publichealth.columbia.edu/news/oil-spill-has-far-reaching-effects-children-families

OECD Data. n.d. *Income Inequality.* Accessed February 5, 2023. www.data.oecd.org/inequality/income-inequity.htm .

Oxford Economics. *Housing has become less affordable across all US metros.* Research Briefing. November 11, 2024. https://www.oxfordeconomics.com/resource/housing-has-become-less-affordable-across-all-us metros/#:~:text=Housing%20affordability%20has%20dropped%20significantly,do%20so%20five%20years%20prior.

Perry, Andre, and David Harshbarger. 2019. "America's Formerly Redlined Neighborhoods Have Changed, And So Must Solutions to Rectify Them." *Bloomberg.* October 14. Accessed December 15, 2022. https://www.brookings.edu/articles/americas-formerly-redlines-areas-changed-so-must-solutions/.

Pew Research Center. 2023. *Public Trust in Government: 1958-2023.* September 19. Accessed October 29, 2023. https://www.pewresearch.org/politics/2023/09/19/public-trust-in-government-1958-2023/.

Piketty, Thomas. 2014. *Capital In The Twenty-First Century.* Cambridge: The Belknap Press of Harvard university Press.

Quadrini, Vincenzo. 2005. "The Importance of Entrepreneur-ship For Wealth Concentration and Mobility." *Review of Income and Wealth.* March 8. Accessed September 30, 2022. https://www.aeequity.org/product/dynastic-wealth-an-approach-to-advancing-racial-equity-in-entre-preneurship-ecosystems.

Redlener, Irwin. 2010. "Oil Spill Has Far-Reaching Effects on Children and Families." *Columbia Mailman School of Public Health.* August 3. Accessed September 18, 2023. https://www.publichealth.columbia.edu/news/oil-spill-has-far-reaching-effects-children-families#:~:text=Sur-vey%20Findings&text=Over%20one%2D-third%20of%20parents,and%208%25%20report%20job%20loss.

Rodriguez Diaz, Abril. 2022. "The Effects of Early Education on Intergenerational Mobility in the United States." *Harvard Undergraduate Economics Review*, September 2.

Romney, Lee. 1999. "Minority-Owned Firm Tend To Hire Within Own Ethnic Group." *Los Angeles Times.* September 18. Accessed October 18, 2023. https://www.latimes.com/arch-ives/la-xpm-1999-sep-18-fi-11575-story.html.

Rose, Heather. 2005. "The Effects of Affirmative Action Pro-grams: Evidence from the university of California at San Diego." *Educational Evaluation and Policy Analysis* (Ameri-can Educational Research Association) 27 (n3): 263-289.

Ross, Glenwood, David Sioquist, and Matthew Wooten. 2008. *Tracking the Economy of the City of Atlanta: Past trends and Future Prospects.* Report, Fiscal Research Center.

Schulman, Carolyn. 2018. *Best Practices for Technical Assistance Programs Serving Black and Hispanic Entrepreneurs and Small Business Owners.* Report, Milken Institute.

Shrider, Emily, "Poverty in the United States: 2023". September 10, 2024. Report No. P60-283. https://www2.census.gov/programs-surveys/cps/techdocs/cpsmar24.pdf.

Shrider, Emily, Melissa Kollar, Frances Chen, and Jessica Semega. 2021. "Income and Poverty in the United States: 2020." *US Census Bureau.* September 14. Accessed December 1, 2022. www.census.gov/topics/income-poverty/income-inequality.html.

State of California. n.d. *About the Program.* Accessed September 23, 2023. https://calosba.ca.gov/funding-grants-incentives/ihub2/#abouttheprogram.

Steverman, Ben. 2022. "America's Inequality Problem Just Improved for the First Time in A Generation." *Bloomberg.* June 8. Accessed January 15, 2023. https://www.bloomberg.com/news/features/2022-06-08/us-income-inequality-fell-during-the-covid-pandemic.

Swope , Carolyn, Diana Hernandez, and Lara Cushing. 2022. "The Relationship of Historical Redlining with Present-Day Neighborhood Environmental and Health Outcomes: A Scoping Review and Conceptual Model." *National Library of Medicine.* August 1. Accessed December 16, 2022. www.ncbi.nlm.nih.gov.

Tax Policy Center Urban Institute & Brookings Institution. n.d. "The Tax Policy Center's Briefing Book." *Tax Policy Center.* Accessed December 13, 2022. www.taxpolicycenter.org.

The Associated Press. 2023. "A New Study Offers Hints That Healthier School Lunches May Help Reduce Obesity." *NPR News.* February 15. Accessed Novemeber 1, 2023. www.npr/2023/02/15/1157176728/healthy-school-means-nutrition-obesity-study.

1787. "The United States Constitution." *National Con-*

stitution Center. September 17. Accessed December 15, 2022. https://constitutioncenter.org/interactive-constitution/white-papers/the-declaration-the-constitution-and-the-bill-of-rights.

U.S. Bureau of Labor Statistics. 2023. "Occupational Outlook Handbook." *U.S. Bureau of Labor Statistics.* September 6. Accessed October 29, 2023. https://www.bls.gov/ooh/math/operations-research-analysts.htm.

U.S. Department of State. 2023. *U.S. Relations With Mexico Bilateral Relations Fact Sheet.* September 13. Accessed October 15, 2023. https://www.state.gov/u-s-relations-with-mexico/#:~:text=In%202021%2C%20U.S.%20goods%20and,2019%20(latest%20data%20available).

U.S. Drug Administration Economic Research Service. n.d. *Documentation.* Accessed November 1, 2023. www.ers.usda.gov/dta-products/food-access-research-atlas/documentation.

U.S. Economic Development Administration. n.d. *i6 Challenge.* Accessed September 22, 2023. https://www.eda.gov/oie/buildtoscale/historical#:~:text=i6%20Challenge%3A%20Launched%20in%202010,creation%2C%20innovation%2C%20and%20commercialization.

United Nations. 2015. "The 2030 Agenda For Sustainable Development." *United Nations.* September 27. Accessed May 20, 2023. www.sustainabledevelopment.un.org.

Walsh, Bryan. 2010. "With Oil Spill (and Blame) Spreading, Obama Will Visit Gulf." *Time.* May 1. Accessed September 18, 2023. https://web.archive.org/web/20100503045805/http://www.time.com/time/health/article/0,8599,1986323,00.html.

Webb, Brittany. *"Can You Hear Me Now?" Middle Class Americans*

Are Priced Out of Housing. Monday, September1, 2025. https://nhc.org/can-you-hear-me-now-middle-class-americans-are-priced-out-of-housing/ #:~:text=The%20findings%20are%20alarming.,purchase %20a%20typically%20priced%20home.

White, LaTanya. *Dynesty Wealth*. https://www.dynas-ticwealth.online/

World Economic Forum. December 10, 2021. Equity, Diversity and Inclusion, "These charts show the growing income inequality between the world's richest and poorest". https://www.weforum.org/agenda/2021/12/global-income-inequaility-gap-report-rich-poor?utm

Xie, Yu, Catherine Massey, Karen Rolf, and Xi Song. 2019. "Long-Term Decline In Intergenerational Mobility in the United States Since the 1850s." *Proceedings of the National Academy of Sciences*, November 25.

---

[1] Juliana Menasce Horowitz, Ruth Igienik and Rakesh Kochhar. "Trends In Income and Wealth Inequality" *Pew Research Center*, January 9 2020. https://www.pewresearch.org/social-trends/2020/01/09/trends-in-income-and-wealth-inequality/ (Menasce Horowitz, Igielnik and Kochhar 2020)

[2] Ibid.

[3] Equity, Diversity and Inclusion, "These charts show the growing income inequality between the world's richest and poorest" World Economic Forum, December 10, 2021. https://www.weforum.org/agenda/2021/12/global-income-inequaility-gap-report-rich-poor?utm

[4] Thomas Piketty, *Capital In The Twenty-First Century* (Cambridge: The Belknap Press of Harvard University Press, 2014). (Piketty 2014)

[5] Bennis, W., & Nanus, B. (1985). *Leaders: The strategies for taking charge*. New York: Harper & Row

[6] "The 2030 Agenda for Sustainable Development." *United Nations*, September 15, 2015. www.sustainabledevelopment.un.org (United Nations 2015)

[7] Farrigan, Tracey. 2021. "Data Show US Poverty Rates in 2019 Higher In Rural Areas Than In Urban For Racial/Ethnic Groups." *Economic Research Service*. August 23. Accessed December 15, 2022. https://www.ers.usda.gov/

data-products/chart-gallery/gallery/chart-detail/?
chartId=101903#:~:text=Data%20show%20U.S.%20pover-
ty%20rates,urban)%20areas%20at%2011.9%20percent

[8] "The United States Constitution" *National Constitution Center*. https://constitutioncenter.org/interactive-constitution/white-papers/the-declaration-the-constitution-and-the-bill-of-rights (The United States Constitution 1787)

[9] Interview held July 31, 2024 in this office 260 14th Street NW Atlanta GA 30318

[10] "About The King Center" *The King Center*. December 15, 2022. www.thekingcenter.org (About The King Center n.d.)

[11] Paul Krugman, "Politics, Policy and Inequality," *Economic Policy Institute*, May 21, 2007. (Krugman 2007)

[12] Carolyn Swope, Diana Hernandez and Lara Cushing. "The Relationship of Historical Redlining with Present-Day Neighborhood Environmental and health Outcomes: A Scoping Review and Conceptual Model". *National Library of Medicine*. August 1, 2022 www.ncbi.nlm.nih.gov (Swope , Hernandez and Cushing 2022)

[13] Ibid.

[14] Andre Perry and David Harshbarger. "America's Formerly Redlined Neighborhoods Have Changed, and So Must Solutions To Rectify Them". *Bloomberg*. October 14, 2019. https://www.brookings.edu/articles/americas-formerly-redlines-areas-changed-so-must-solutions/ (Perry and Harshbarger 2019)

[15] "Japanese American Incarceration," The National WWII Museum New Orleans, https://www.nationalww2museum.org/war/articles/japanese-american-incarceration (Japanese American Incarceration n.d.)

[16] Colin Gordon. "Growing Apart: A Political History of American Inequality" *Differences That Matter*, April 6, 2020. www.scalar.usc.edu (Growing Apart: A Politcal History of American Inequality 2020)

[17] Ibid.

[18] "The Tax Policy Center's Briefing Book," Tax Policy Center. www.taxpolicycenter.org (Tax Policy Center Urban Institute & Brookings Institution n.d.)

[19] Ben Steverman. "America's Inequality Problem Just Improved for the First Time in a Generation," *Bloomberg*, June 2022, https://www.bloomberg.com/news/features/2022-06-08/us-income-inequality-fell-during-the-covid-pandemic

[20] Ibid.

(Steverman 2022)

[21] Emily Shrider, Melissa Kollar, Frances Chen and Jessica Semega, "Income and Poverty in the United States: 2020" *US Census Bureau*, September 14, 2021. https://www.census.gov/topics/income-poverty/income-inequality.html (Shrider, et al. 2021)

[22] Tracey Farrigan, "Data Show US Poverty Rates in 2019 Higher In Rural Areas Than In Urban for Racial/Ethic Groups." *US Department of Agriculture.* August 23, 2021. https://www.ers.usda.gov/data-products/chart-gallery/gallery/chart-detail/?chartId=101903#:~:text=Data%20show%20U.S.%20poverty%20rates,urban)%20areas%20at%2011.9%20percent.

[23] Shrider, Emily, "Poverty in the United States: 2023". September 10, 2024. Report No. P60-283. https://www2.census.gov/programs-surveys/cps/techdocs/cpsmar24.pdf.

[24] Sarah Clark and Gary Freed, "Teen Involvement in Demonstrations Against Policy Brutality" *Mott Poll Report* Vol. 37 Issue 2 (2020) 1-2 https://mottpoll.org/reports?page=2 (Clark and Freed 2020)

[25] Nicholas Kristof. "Pull Yourself Up By Bootstraps? Go Ahead, Try It," *New York Times* Feb 19, 2020. (Kristof 2020)

[26] Heather Rose. "The Effects of Affirmative Action Programs: Evidence from the University of California at San Diego," *Educational Evaluation and Policy Analysis*, v27 n3 p 263-289 Fall 2005 https://eric.ed.gov/?id=EJ737166 (Rose 2005)

[27] Jay Bailey, https://russellcenter.org/about-us/. Retrieved November 8, 2025.

[28] "Occupational Outlook Handbook" *US Bureau of Labor Statistics.* September 6, 2023 https://www.bls.gov/ooh/math/operations-research-analysts.htm. October 29, 2023. (U.S. Bureau of Labor Statistics 2023)

[29] Eric Belsky. "Lack of Access to Financial Services Impedes Economic Mobility," *Federal Reserve Bank of Atlanta.* October 16, 2018. https://www.atlantafed.org/economy-matters/community-and-economic-development/2018/10/16/lack-of-access-to-financial-services-impedes-economic-mobility (Belsky 2018)

[30] Lee Romney. "Minority-Owned Firms Tend to Hire Within Own Ethic Group," *LA Times.* September 18, 1999. https://www.latimes.com/archives/la-xpm-1999-sep-18-fi-11575-story.html. October 28, 2023. (Romney 1999)

[31] Ibid

[32] Brittany Webb. *"Can You Hear Me Now?" Middle Class Americans Are Priced Out of Housing.* Monday, September1, 2025. https://nhc.org/can-you-hear-me-now-middle-class-americans-are-priced-out-of-housing/

#:~:text=The%20findings%20are%20alarming.,purchase%20a%20typically
%20priced%20home.

[33] Oxford Economics. *Housing has become less affordable across all US metros.*
Research Briefing. November 11, 2024. https://www.oxfordeconomics.com/
resource/housing-has-become-less-affordable-across-all-us-metros/
#:~:text=Housing%20affordability%20has%20dropped%20significantly,do
%20so%20five%20years%20prior.

[34] Margarita Herrejon, *Equity: Person Centric*, Illustration, Atlanta, GA 2023
(Herrejon 2023)

[35] *Small Business Technical Assistance Micro Business, Small Business and
Business Expansion.* https://communityactionpartnership.com/wp-content/
uploads/2018/06/small-business-technical-assistance.pdf

[36] Carolyn Karo and Jackson Mueller. *Partnership For Lending in Underserved
Markets.* September, 2017. https://milkeninstitute.org/sites/default/files/re-
ports-pdf/092617-PLUM-Phase-I-Summary.pdf

[37] How Credit Scores Can Transform a Community, CEO John Hope Bryant
Operation Hope Channel. October 6, 2022. (Bryant 2022)

[38] Michael Jarand and Kevin Klowden, "Rebuilding California's Trade Policy
Infrastructure," *Milken Institute*, May 12, 2019. https://milkeninstitute.org/
sites/default/files/reports-pdf/Rebuilding-Californias-Trade-Policy-
Infrastructure-FINAL_0.pdf (Jarand and Klowden 2019)

[39] Claudia, Deane. *Americans Deeping Mistrust of Institutions.* October 17,
2024. https://www.pew.org/en/trend/archive/fall-2024/americans-deepen-
ing-mistrust-of-
institutions#:~:text=Americans'%20trust%20in%20the%20federal,ad-
equately%20careful%20with%20taxpayer%20money.

[40] Federal Deposit Insurance Corporation, 2023 FDIC National Survey of
Unbanked and Underbanked Households. https://www.fdic.gov/household-
survey/2023-fdic-national-survey-unbanked-and-underbanked-households-
report

[41] Dr. LaTanya White. *Dynesty Wealth.* https://www.dynasticwealth.online/

[42] Ibid.

[43] Glenwood Ross, David L Sjoquist and Matthew Wooten. "Tracking the
Economy of the City of Atlanta: Past trends and Future Prospects," *Fiscal Research Center Report* No. 176 May 2008. (Ross, Sioquist and Wooten 2008)

[44] "Income Inequality" *OECD Data.* www.data.oecd.org/inequality/income-
inequity.htm February 5, 2023 (OECD Data n.d.)

[45] Dylan Jackson."Atlanta has the highest income inequality in the nation,
Census data shows," *Atlanta Journal Constitution.* November 28, 2022 (Jackson
2022)

[46] Nikolai Elneser, *Race and Income*, Atlanta, Neighborhood Nexus. November 1, 2023 (Elneser 2021)

[47] "Documentation" U.S. Drug Administration Economic Research Service. November 1, 2023. www.ers.usda.gov/dta-products/food-access-research-atlas/documentation (U.S. Drug Administration Economic Research Service n.d.)

[48] "A New Study Offers Hints that Healthier School. Lunches May Help Reduce Obesity" *The Associated Press.* February 15, 2023. www.npr/2023/02/15/1157176728/healthy-school-means-nutrition-obesity-study. November 1, 2023. (The Associated Press 2023)

[49] Ibid.

[50] "Atlanta Region Adds 64,400 Residents in Past Year, ARC Population

Estimates Show" Atlanta Regional Commission. August 13, 2025.

https://atlantaregional.org/news/press-releases/atlanta-region-adds-64400-residents-in-past-year-arc-population-estimates-show/#:~:text=The%20region's%20growth%20is%20being,Las%20Vegas%2C%20Houston%20and%20Miami.

[51] Megan Feldman. "New Harvard Study Reveals Lasting Benefits of Quality Early Childhood Education," *First Five Years Fund.* March 23, 2018. https://www.ffyf.org/new-harvard-study-reveals-lasting-benefits-quality-early-childhood-education/ (Feldman 2018)

[52] Abril Rodriguez Diaz. "The Effects of Early Education on Intergenerational Mobility In the United States," *Harvard Undergraduate Economics Review.* September 2, 2022. https://www.economicsreview.org/post/the-effects-of-early-education-on-intergenerational-mobility-in-the-united-states (Rodriguez Diaz 2022)

[53] Bhash. Mazumder. "Intergenerational Economic Mobility in the United States". Policy Brief, April 2022. Chicago Federal Reserve. https://www.chicagofed.org/research/content-areas/mobility/intergenerational-economic-mobility#:~:text=In%20more%20recent%20work%2C%20my,downward%20mobility%20from%20the%20top.

[54] "Who We Are" *Communities in School.* https://www.cislosangeles.org/mission.html , September 23, 2023. (Communities in Schools n.d.)

[55] "Education, Income, and Wealth (Page One Economics)," *Federal Reserve of St. Louis.* January, 2017 https://www.stlouisfed.org/en/education/page-one-economics-classroom-edition/education-income-and-wealth (Federal Reserve Bank of St. Louis n.d.)

[56] Tony Cardenas, Karen Bass and Cory Booker. "Second Chance For Justice Juvenile Justice And Criminal Justice Package," 2019. https://cardenas.house.gov/imo/media/doc/

Second%20Chance%20for%20Justice%20Package.pdf (Cardenas, Bass and Booker 2019)

[57] Ibid.

[58] Chris Metinko. "Venture Fell More Than 40% In Hottest States For Funding," *Crunchbase News*. January 27, 2023. https://news.crunchbase.com/venture/startup-funding-california-massachusetts-new-york/ (Metinko 2023)

[59] Guest Commentary. "R&D Investments Drive California Innovation," *Cal Matters*. February 18, 2022. https://calmatters.org/commentary/2022/02/rd-investments-drive-california-innovation/ (Commentary 2022)

[60] Leonard Mitchell, Deepak Bahl and Nicholas Busalacchi. "iHub California Innovation Hub" *USC Center for Economic Development on behalf of U.S. Department of Commerce, Economic Development Administration*. December, 2013. https://bpb-us-e1.wpmucdn.com/sites.usc.edu/dist/e/242/files/2023/01/California-Innovation-Hub-iHub-Profiles-and-Indicators-2013-1twhj1x.pdf (Mitchell, Bahl and Busalacchi 2013)

[61] "About the Program" *Accelerate California Inclusive Innovation Hubs*. September 23, 2023. https://calosba.ca.gov/funding-grants-incentives/ihub2/#abouttheprogram (State of California n.d.)

[62] "i6 Challenge" *U.S. Economic Development Administration*. September 22, 2023. https://www.eda.gov/oie/buildtoscale/historical#:~:text=i6%20Challenge%3A%20Launched%20in%202010,creation%2C%20innovation%2C%20and%20commercialization (U.S. Economic Development Administration n.d.)

[63] Ibid.

[64] Ibid.

[65] "Oil Spill Has Far-Reaching Effects on Children and

Families", Columbia University. August 3, 2010

https://www.publichealth.columbia.edu/news/oil-spill-has-far-reaching-effects-children-families

[66] Jens Manuel Krogstad, Jeffrey Passel, Mohamad Moslimani and Luis Noe-Bustamente. "Key Facts About U.S. Latinos For National Hispanic Heritage Month" *Pew Research Center*. September 22, 2023. https://www.pewresearch.org/short-reads/2022/09/23/key-facts-about-u-s-latinos-for-national-hispanic-heritage-month/#:~:text=People%20of%20Mexican%20origin%20accounted,the%20island%20as%20of%202021). (krogstad, et al. 2023)

[67] Jesus Canas and Chloe Smith. "Investment in Mexico Falls Despite Rise in Remittances" Federal Reserve Bank of Dallas. June 29, 2021. https://www.dallasfed.org/research/economics/2021/0629 (Canas and Smith 2021)

[68] "Money Mexican Migrants Send Home Up 13.4% in 2022" Associated Press. February 1, 2023. https://apnews.com/article/caribbean-mexico-city-business-050ef97bc5255b4339d31fed39ed14a0 (Associated Press 2023)

[69] Ibid.

[70] " U.S. Relations With Mexico: Bilateral Relations," *U.S. Department of State.* September 13, 2023. https://www.state.gov/u-s-relations-with-mexico/#:~:text=In%202021%2C%20U.S.%20goods%20and,2019%20(latest%20data%20available). October 15, 2023. (U.S. Department of State 2023)

ABOUT THE AUTHOR

Dr. Eloisa Klementich

 Dr. Eloisa Klementich is President and CEO of Invest Atlanta, where she leads efforts to create a more equitable and prosperous city. With over 20 years of experience in economic and community development at local, state, national, and international levels, she has helped drive billions in investment, thousands of jobs and affordable housing units in Atlanta. Guided by a deep passion for building inclusive communities and a vision of economic opportunity for all, Dr. Klementich is known for her hands-on approach and her unwavering commitment to making a difference in people's lives. Dr. Klementich has served as the President of the International Economic Development Council and holds advanced degrees from Pitzer College, UCLA, Tecnologico de Monterrey and the University of LaVerne, and has received numerous awards for her leadership and impact.

PRAISE FOR AUTHOR

"Discovering programs and initiatives that can empower the lives of everyday community members is always worth learning from. Dr. Klementich's book offers just this type of insight. Her passion and commitment to revitalization and the creation of wealth provides a path to feeding the hungry, clothing the naked, healing the sick and housing the homeless."

- AMBASSADOR ANDREW YOUNG

"Eloisa's seminal book An Equity Blueprint is a must-have for any policymaker, community organizer, or institutional leader seeking creative ways to create deep-rooted, lasting change, especially at the local level. As both the child of immigrant parents from diverse backgrounds coming of age in a rapidly changing America, and as the leader of one of Atlanta's biggest drivers of economic development and community change-making, Eloisa is uniquely qualified to lead us in such a transformative conversation.

The implications of this text are many, chief among them is that conversation alone is insufficient. Action—on some level—must accompany the theoretical solutions we offer, and she has demonstrated this with her leadership at Invest Atlanta.

As we stand at a crossroads in our nation's history, we must all lean in, locate ourselves in the challenges we face collectively, and assess how we can all begin doing our part to develop meaningful solutions. *Equity At Scale* reminds us that equality is only the beginning. Equity is the solution that raises the standard and ensures an America that works for us all and equips people with the tools they need to thrive and succeed."

- JOHN HOPE BRYANT, FOUNDER, CHAIRMAN AND CEO OPERATION HOPE

"In *The Equity Blueprint*, Klementich, a highly respected Atlanta leader, provides a practical blueprint to address systematic inequities that plague cities throughout the country. The book shares her remarkable experience designing public, philanthropic and private funding models to close equity gaps in crucial housing, healthcare and core business development deals that offers basic resources for families to thrive. The book should be required reading for academics and municipal leadership seeking proven collaborative models that deliver efficient equity to drive long-term positive impact."

- MARGARET STAGMEIER

AUTHOR "BLIGHTED: THE STORY OF PEOPLE, POLITICS AND AN AMERICAN HOUSING MIRACLE"

"Congratulations to Eloisa Klementich on the release of *The Equity Blueprint*! At the Urban League of Greater Atlanta, we believe this book arrives at a pivotal moment. Its actionable strategies and visionary approach provide a roadmap for advancing equity in ways that strengthen people, communities and create lasting opportunities for all. In these times, when inclusive growth and shared prosperity are more critical than ever, this work can inspire leaders and organizations to drive meaningful change. We applaud Eloisa's commitment and encourage everyone to explore this important resource. "

- NANCY FLAKE JOHNSON, PRESIDENT & CEO, URBAN LEAGUE OF GREATER ATLANTA

"Dr. Klementich's career has consistently placed her at the intersection of many of the issues she addresses in the book. She shines a light on the depth and complexity of these issues, and challenges us all to engage in the broad-based partnerships required to build strong communities, the foundation of a strong nation."

- EGBERT PERRY, CHAIRMAN & CEO OF THE INTEGRAL GROUP